Deepak Loomba, is Founder-Director of AICorps EPL. Invention of Description is a path-breaking methodology, invented and applied by the author.

This short, to-the-point book provides an understanding of the methodology along with real life applications.

The methodology allowed the author to create a conveyor of innovations, while ensuring that young and amateur colleagues created products and services with quality that competes with the products designed by the wisest and most experienced designers.

Compelling read for everyone from an engineer to a house-maker, who want to assess quality – of anything, from relationships to food and the most high technology products or services. For young, who are sculpting a start-up enterprise, the methodology assists in circumventing mistakes that their peers often made.

INVENTION OF DESCRIPTION

Path-breaking methodology of description of quality

ISBN: 9798636521334

First published in June 2017

SCAN QR TO LEAVE REVIEWS

Preface

Invention of Description is an introduction to the methodology invented by the author for creating a description of tangibles as well as intangibles.

Through research undertaken in the field of quality and description, the author to the best of his knowledge, found no equivalence to **DNSEA** methodology, which has been elaborated in 'Invention of Description'.

Dedicated to my Father-in-law, Mr. Hardipender Singh, a Civil Engineer and a practicing Advocate, who inculcated in me a spirit of critical evaluation towards oneself, things & events around oneself.

Very Special Mention:

- A special mention is to be made of my immensely inspiring father Mr. Ved Prakash Loomba.

- Cheers & thanks to my wife Harsh, an expressive and original fine artist (painter) and my son Mehul, now an undergraduate student specializing in the field of Mechatronics. Both love me and stand by me in camaraderie.

- A special mention of my professor Glasko from Moscow State University, who taught me Mathematical Analysis, such that it became a part of me and not only formed the basis of **DNSEA**, but also helped me solve a number of complex riddles in business and philosophy.

Background to Invention of Description

Invention of Description was an idea that was born from a bid to understand quality.

One of the questions that troubled me for long was - whether quality is subjective or objective? Subjective, here means that which is relatively different for every human being in experience, while objective being universally same when experienced by all people.

The issue gained criticality in the process of establishing a quality policy for one of our companies. In conclusion of detour of many books, ideas and thoughts that I immersed myself in, I came to a few conclusions. These conclusions assisted me in inventing description – which I termed as **DNSEA**, such that 'D' stands for description, 'N' for the necessary attributes or conditions, 'S' for sufficiency attributes or conditions, 'E' for emotional connect and 'A' for aesthetic value. The reader of this book who implements **DNSEA** shall be able to provide full description of anything tangible or intangible. It is critically important for those who are involved in product development or research as it will help them to understand their query as well as the results much better when studied through implementation of the said methodology.

DNSEA therefore is one of the many methodologies of describing objects, processes and phenomena, but one, which provides a complete description of whatsoever desired from a marriage to food in a restaurant.

Contents

1. DNSEA

The acronym DNSEA stands for following:

'**D**' stands for Description,

'**N**' stands for Necessary Attributes or Conditions,

'**S**' stands for Sufficiency Attributes or Conditions,

'**E**' stands for Attributes of Emotional Connect

'**A**' stands for Aesthetic Attributes

Having spent many evenings through the year 2011-2012 thinking & reading about Quality, I felt that a generic & functional definition of Quality was hop-skipping me. I wanted to create a concept of quality that comprehensively described quality of tangibles and intangibles, while being all-encompassing. The concept should leave no quality attribute unaddressed. It is worthwhile mentioning, that through the last 4 years of hiring from various best institutes both business management and top science ones, as also various people with experience, not one answered my following question correctly – Is Quality objective or subjective? Fresh college recruits after some thought answered incorrectly – "subjective". Few of them answered "objective". Truth as always lies in the middle. Quality of anything tangible or intangible has both subjective as well as objective components to it. But this understanding came to me with time and effort and not spontaneously. Through this book, I shall discuss all these various aspects of **DNSEA**. It is important to note that in the process of creation of this concept I realized that Quality of anything (tangible or intangible) needs a methodological description, which is generic and does not vary depending on the object of description. **DNSEA** is such a methodology. This realization happened after lot of experiencing and consequent thinking. In the next chapter, I provide my readers the reason for the birth of this concept.

2.   Hiring

Hiring is a difficult task. When I started my enterprise in 2009-2010 I had a team of few core people in place, but I had to hire a few more immediately – including a Company Secretary, a Chartered Accountant, HR personnel etc.

Scoring without standardization - a mirage

In the process of hiring, two or three of us would interview people. We decided to give score on a scale of 10 to every interviewee. I observed that for the same person each one of us would give very different scores. Sometimes, grossly divergent. This struck me as strange. We were interviewing same people, and gauging them on same parameters, how then can there be so divergent views on aspects, which should ideally be objective. I realized that one of the reasons for this divergence is the disparity in perception of evaluation parameters/criteria/attributes of the interviewers. It was apparent that some common parameters needed to be evolved among us. I had no immediate solution on hand, as I remained occupied with other critical tasks, nevertheless, the issue stuck in my mind for long. How to have a generic system ensuring congruence among evaluators, so that the attributes evaluated are easily understood; as also the rating/scoring system.

While I was living with the aforementioned wish without any major resolution, a new task cropped up a few months later, unconnected with aforementioned travails. We decided to become an ISO 9001 certified company. In the process, one of my colleagues informed that we have to settle on a quality policy. On one of the late evenings, I was still at work along with three other colleagues, one of whom was my product designer (a young, high-yield, chain smoker with attitude & ideas). He passed by my office, while I was discussing the following day tasks with my Executive Assistant Calling him in I asked him to define quality. A split second later he started to explain something. I intervened in-between, cutting him short, I exhalted him to frame a definition. He retorted, "Sir, then give me some time & I come back to you." It must have been about 40minutes later that he came in & said that on research and thought, he concluded that anything of good quality has three attributes – it is fit for the purpose it is done, people feel an emotional connect to it and it is aesthetic.

I liked all that he said, but for the "fit for purpose" part, I felt that the bar dropped too low. I argued, "if I ask you to make a skateboard or a cycle for me to travel to the market place, few kilometers away, peddling; would it be a good idea to make a cardboard or cheap soft wood cycle, which might serve my purpose of peddling to the market but will fail to let me peddle back?" "Secondly, when we talk about emotional connect," I added, "whose emotional connect is one talking about?"

In following days, on finer thinking, I realized that humankind has a tendency to manufacture goods that live and are usable for long. The only exception being products designed for single use – disposable cups to surgical gloves. There is a certain underlying spontaneity towards conservation of resources. This largely stems from inclination of mankind to adopt the path of least resistance. The concept of least resistance is applicable in this context because production of resources requires substantial amount of human labour. Therefore, there is proclivity towards conversation of resources that is - expend least amount of human labour. Indeed, inclination of resource wastage is directly proportional to automation & economic prosperity of a society.

Therefore, I decided in my mind that 'fit for purpose' has to be replaced with two conditionalities, which like in mathematical analysis are necessary & sufficient. Necessary conditions or necessary attributes are 'fit for targeted purpose', besides being 'safe' in production, storage and use. I still was lost on the sufficiency attributes/conditions. I must have kept on pondering over it for a few days, without any respite or resolution.

The other question that popped in my mind was - What if the necessary conditions are satisfied, but sufficient conditions are not? What would we say of quality then? I realized quality has to be rated based on a generic definition. Must have been a few weeks later, that I gradually generated a definition of quality. In the meanwhile, that very evening along with my product designer and executive assistant, we finalized the Quality Policy of our Co. – it is

"We, personally commit to swiftly create, deliver, and continuously improve – innovation, State-of-the-Art design and reliability."

For the next few weeks, I kept on thinking about quality definition that would answer my questions - including the one on sufficiency attributes/conditions, though the ISO requirements were already accomplished.

A few weeks of thinking, gradually, helped me generate sufficiency conditions for defining quality description.

Here is the bonus - in the process of inventing the description of quality, I realized, I had also resolved the problem of generic system of scoring (evaluation), which provided needed objectivity to every assessment that was made thereafter.

3.   Categorization & Assessment

After many days of thought experiments, hits and trials, I concluded on the final definition of quality – thereby simultaneously 'inventing the description'.

Objective and the Subjective

The next keel on which I rest my methodology is that a complete description should have both the objective and subjective. In the context of this book,

'Objective' is quantitatively &/or qualitatively affirmed by everyone experiencing it (similarly) & remains unchanged on repeated assessments within a reasonable timeframe.

'Subjective' is that whose assessment differs from person to person, although the object or subject of assessment is the same and is being assessed within a reasonable timeframe.

I have often questioned interviewees as to whether quality according to them is subjective or objective. As soon as one decides to choose, one goes wrong. Reality is that quality has both the objective and subjective aspects. The objective, because they are experienced similarly by all, are necessary to adhere to, while the subjective define the life and economics of the input/output being assessed for quality. A good strategy is to objectivize the subjective, to the extent possible. One way to objectivize the subjective is by acquiring subjective assessments and in case an overwhelming majority concurs in their subjective assessment, one can pronounce the said subjective assessment as statistically objective. An example is – analysis of 'liking' of a painting. Liking needs no justification or reasoning, and is hence completely subjective. Show 500 people a painting and ask if they like it or not, if an overwhelming majority confirms, one can categorize the painting as aesthetically beautiful (universal liking). Aesthetics is nothing but universal, statistically affirmed 'liking'. Hence, becoming quasi-objective, as a result.

Assessment - umbilical cord of quality & Description

Description is the process of converting fruitful data into information for memorizing.

Epistemologically, this is how humans store knowledge.

I discovered for myself that description of anything consists of two parts. The order in which, each of these parts are expressed is determined by the language used. Two parts of description are:

a)	Categorization, thereby making it convenient to assess, treat and compare.

b)	Assessment of various attributes, their fields, amplitudes (or values) and directions.

For description, categorization has to be done foremost. It is inductive & important because all assessment have a comparative constituent. To ensure an apple to an apple comparison, good categorization is necessary.

Categorization

Categorization is nothing but a sorting on the fly. Such that most of one's life is spent learning and memorizing various categories (like baskets), into which we humans instantaneously throw every presented specimen.

For procuring a statistical (objective) understanding of the innovativeness of the resource assessed as well as its repeat usage. This unremitting vote/inquiry along with a vote on emotional connect with the resource, indicates some very critical features of the assessed resource, when studied in combination of absolute and comparative emotional connect and aesthetic value. This category therefore, has to be perennially present irrespective of other categorizations.

The value of this Field is quaternion[1] –

(i)   Yes,   (ii)   Yes, Re-experiencing this

(iii)   No,   (iv)   No, Re-experiencing this

Re-experience means that the assessed resource has been consumed previously by Effected-Entities (consumer/user).

Assessment

Assessment requires evaluation of the input/output (resource) in four frameworks – (i) Necessary Attributes Framework; (ii) Sufficiency Attributes Framework; (iii) Emotional Connect Framework; (iv) Aesthetic Attributes Framework. Necessary Attributes' Framework is the carrier of objectivity. Sufficiency Attributes' Framework is the determinant of life of resources, with at least one objective constraint. The other constraint may indeed be subjective. Emotional Connect Framework has two Fields the absolute and the comparative

---

[1] That which can assume four values

both being completely subjective. The last one is Aesthetic Framework, which is objective as it is cast from statistics accumulated from assessment of emotional connect of various people. Deeper understanding of each of these shall follow. Each of the discovered frameworks and fields constituting them are hurdled-ranked[2] in priority/order mentioned above. To understand these frameworks and their origin, I propose to commence with the second framework – that of Sufficiency Attributes. This is because in this framework is embodied with a component titled 'ownership', which is important to be understood for clarity on other three frameworks.

Assessment in the Sufficiency Framework

Assessment of Sufficiency has three components - Fields, Values & Directions. Each field could have multiple attributes/indicators/aspects on which the subject or object of assessment is measured and each of these attributes may have either value or direction or both of them.

Fields

These are dimensions of assessment. Like Einstein frame of reference, fields too are four types. First field is Ownership (this is the observer, user, orderer, participant or impact bearer of change - the conscious agent, on whose behalf parameters for other three fields are set, who is foremost impacted by change in the attributes of the assessed resource and a change in whom leads to changes in assessed attributes

---

[2] Hurdle-ranking in context of our book is - treatment of each field of each framework as a ranked (in priority) hurdle, such that the description of the resource is considered to be of the rank, previous in order to the hurdle not crossed.

of all other fields). The second field is Quantitative Field, third field is Qualitative field and the fourth and last field is that of Geo-ambience. Furthermore, each of these four fields occur in a pre-determined sequence. That is ownership, quantitative, qualitative, geo-ambience.

The discovery of these four fields (/dimensions) of assessment is coupled to baring of related facts in my other book 'Awareness and Consciousness – The New Upanishad' (ISBN: 978-1692201227, ASIN: B07XQ3BMF1).

Origin of Fields

To understand origin of fields, consider a universe, hundred percent, strictly spontaneous. Spontaneity in context of this book is unambiguous and defined as that which is fully concurrent with the laws of entropy. Such a spontaneous universe deems no need of an observer, as there is no change that can be effected in the course of nature, else the law of entropy (spontaneity, natural flow of energy, distribution of chaos) be disturbed. Any such universe will flow without any need of a conscious agent. This is what the world would be if 'we' along with all consciousness of the universe suddenly annihilate.

Enters - non-spontaneity, something that disturbs the course of entropy. This first non-spontaneous event or occurrence was the evolution of the most primitive form of 'conscious-agent' or 'observer' (in context of this book, observer and conscious-agent are interchangeable and indicate one and the same). It is only with occurrence or appearance of the observer that the other three fields of assessment arise. Until observer is non-existent, so is the need or cause of assessment.

Therefore, ownership (observer / conscious-agent) is the origin of all assessments, including the other three fields.

Interestingly, very similar scientific conclusions are reached by quantum science, though in reverse. Quantum science claims that the presence of an observer itself ignites a non-spontaneous change (Observer Effect). My conclusion takes a different route reaching Everest from the other side. Keeping non-spontaneity as an event, I have concluded it as the moment of origin of an observer or conscious agent. I have outlined a step-by-step evolution of non-spontaneity from spontaneity in my book 'Awareness and Consciousness – The New Upanishad' (ISBN: 978-1692201227, ASIN: B07XQ3BMF1).

Now imagine a universe of nothingness with an observer and one single particle (or point). Simultaneous with the origin of the first particle (or point), Quantitative Field springs up. The observer can place himself in a coordinate system that originates from the particle. Thereby, ascertaining his own position in the coordinates. But a universe with single particle will still have no Qualitative Field – there is nothing to compare or interact with. Even if the observer assumes that the single particle has magnetic or electric properties, there is no way he can confirm or negate, as any such property requires interaction with another particle. If not an interaction, then at least a comparison. It is only of another particle has no magnetic properties, can the first one be termed magnetic. Difference in assessed values creates functional relationships, even if mathematical.

It is therefore, on appearance of second particle that connectivity, interaction, comparison amongst the two particles happen. Giving way to evolution of Qualitative Field. This field is one of properties, most of which happen owing to interaction among the particles.

The third field is that of geo-ambience. This is quite like a tensor field. It informs the location, environs and interaction of the object (or subject) of assessment with its environs at the said location. This therefore is a field, which indicates the position and local conditions, thereby, allowing & appreciating non-uniformity in the field. Would a field be uniform all over, there would be no need to assess local conditions.

Values

When an object (or subject) is assessed for its value at a specific moment. One gets a spot value - that is, the amplitude of the assessed attribute of the field at a specific point of time. This is termed as the 'Value' of attribute.

Direction

When repeated instantaneous Value assessments are made vis-à-vis specific points of time, one gets a dynamic of the values. This generates the direction of change of the assessed values of an attribute. Assessment is a comparative study of various attributes of the assessed object (or subject) in their value and direction. The table below vividly explains Assessment.

SN	Field	Value	Direction
1	Ownership (observer, conscious agent, effecting and effected entity when the observer or attributes of other fields change in value or direction)	Nomenclature or value of observer	Direction of Change in observation
2	Quantitative attributes	Values of attribute	Direction of change
3	Qualitative attributes		
4	Geo-ambience attributes		

From the understanding provided in the last section of Assessment in Sufficiency Attributes' framework we know that the observer's / user's / orderer's / participant's / Impact-bearer's (conscious-agents) position is fundamental and vital for all 'Fields' of assessment, as the constraints in the other three Fields are guided by this one.

From this presence of a conscious agent arises the other three Frameworks of Assessment.

The first in order of ranking is Necessary Attributes' Framework. It has two sub-categories – 'Safety First' & 'Fitness'. Though in order of ranking Safety precedes Fitness, yet conceptually for understanding risks better, we first focus on Fitness.

Assessment in Necessary Attributes' Framework - Fitness related attributes

Fitness has four Fields with Values, but no direction. Because Fitness stands for the spot measurement value of the attribute being assessed. Therefore, change that the attribute undergoes with time is not dealt with, in Fitness Attributes. Dynamics & attributes and consequent change is dealt with, only in Sufficiency Attributes' Framework.

Fitness

Fitness in context of our Book/Concept means – fulfillment of the reason for which something is done or exists. Generally, there are fitness parameters within which something has to fit. But in rare cases the requirement is reversed – of zero fitness or lack of fitness. Most of such cases are those which assess negative valence generating circumstances. A good example would be – describing people who do not suffer from COVID 19 viral infection – in such case the fitness parameter is absence of sore throat. In such case we define a fitness condition, whose absence is the desired / ideal condition.

Fitness has four fields:

(i)   Fitness by purpose;
(ii)   Fitness in time;
(iii)   Fitness in geo-ambience;
(iv)   Fitness in cost.

Fitness-for-purpose Field

Fitness-for-purpose is the reason for which a resource is created or exists and in some rare cases – essential absence of purpose all together. Purpose is defined by the conscious agent which could an individual, an entity (group of individuals), or could even be public at large.

Fitness-in-geoambience Field

It represents the suitability of a resource's existence and use, vis-à-vis the place & ambience in which it is used/proposed-to-be-used from the conscious-agents'[3] standpoint. In some rare cases – suitability is defined by essential absence of certain stipulated geo-ambience conditions.

Fitness-by-time Field

It represents the suitability of time of a resource's existence and use/proposed-use; from the conscious-agents'[4] standpoint. In some rare cases – suitability is defined by essential non-occurrence of specific resources (incl. events/phenomena) at some specific pre-determined time or duration.

Fitness-by-cost Field

It represents the suitability of economic cost of a resource used/proposed-to-be-used from the conscious-agents'[5] standpoint. In some rare cases such suitability is defined by mandatory absence/impossibility of assessment of cost of resource. This element needs the conscious agent because suitability of price is a comparative exercise. Price for any goods or services is derived from how many customers will be ready to pay what for it, keeping in mind the minimum

---

[3] Conscious agent in context of this book is the observer(s) / user(s) / orderer(s) / participant(s) / Impact-bearer(s) and in some cases it includes public-at-large.

[4] Conscious agent in context of this book is the observer(s) / user(s) / orderer(s) / participant(s) / Impact-bearer(s) and in some cases it includes public-at-large.

[5] Conscious agent in context of this book is the observer(s) / user(s) / orderer(s) / participant(s) / Impact-bearer(s) and in some cases it includes public-at-large.

quantity below which it is technically not possible to produce. The customer's point of view gains vitality because he will seek to compare the prices with an anologue.

All the aforementioned fitness fields are binary because that is how fitness exists. Everything under assessment is either fit or not. There is no intermediate state, in which the field is 'not-so-fit' or 'not-completely-unfit'. Fitness relates to a condition of unambiguous surpassing of the barrier of necessary conditions.

Safety related attributes is the other element of Assessment in Necessary Attributes' Framework, but for thorough understanding Safety (Risks & uncertainty) it is important to first understand the Concept of Resources, as propounded by me. Therefore, I have dedicated the next two Chapters to understanding what I term Unified Theory of Resources. Safety Attributes of assessment follow these two chapters on resources.

Additionally, in the next few sub-sections of the current chapter, I discuss other interesting and vital aspects of Assessment.

Assessment and Linguistics

As discovered in previous sub-section description of anything consists of (a) Categorization, thereby making it convenient to assess, treat and compare & (b) Assessment of various attributes, their fields, values (or amplitudes) and direction of change.

A priori it can be induced that categorization has to precede assessment. This is so because assessment is dependent on categorization. When one uses the phrase bad pen. One first categorizes the object in the class of 'pens' and only then on comparing various variants from the same class of pens can one make a conclusion of classifying a specific pen – 'bad pen'.

Since assessment depends on causation of categorization, latter has to precede former to abide by the Law of Causality. This is so, when it comes to the root process of thinking. But how it is expressed linguistically might differ dramatically.

In many languages of the world, assessment precedes categorization in chronology, indicating that the said linguistic tradition ensures / enforces thought to precede speech, reasonably in advance.

Would one be speaking parallel to thinking – that is simultaneously; categorization (generally, using nouns) is done first, followed by assessment (adjectives).

A good example is - we first observe whether the person in front of us is a man or a woman and only then do we analyze good looking or not he (or she) is.

In some languages of the world (I know Hindi, Punjabi and Russian), adjectives precede nouns and are transformed to be in rhythm with latter. Would speech be concurrent to thought, this behavioural element indicates retroduction or abductive-reasoning[6]. An example would be two gender

---

[6] Abductive reasoning is a form of logical inference which starts with an observation or set

dependent Hindi phrases 'bardaa ladka' (big boy) & bardee ladki (big girl). Adjective suffixes are transformed to rhythm better with noun. In thought chronology – thought of noun (classification, whether the seen person is boy or girl) has to be precede adjective (comparative assessment within the class). This is so because adjective is dependent on noun. In other words, noun is the cause of transformation of the adjective's suffix. Abidance to laws of causality makes it apparent that all humans first think noun, which cause relevant change in the adjective's suffix. But in expression style (of Russian, Hindi, Punjabi) nouns are following the adjective. Furthermore, the suffix of the adjective is transformed phonetically to accord with the sound of the noun that follows. It is thus implied, that in Hindi, Russian, Punjabi, humans reverse the thought order of nouns preceding adjectives to getting adjectives to precede nouns when expressed. Therefore, it can be implied that humans speaking Hindi or Russian have to first think both the noun and the adjective, then cognize, then reverse the order and only thereafter speak them. Thus providing a reasonable time to perceive thoughts, before them being uttered.

English embodies higher equity. It does not distinguish between genders and does not transform the adjective depending on the gender of the noun. Good is used as it is, for both boys and girls.

---

of observations and then seeks to find the simplest and most likely explanation for the observations. This process, unlike deductive reasoning, yields a plausible conclusion but does not positively verify it.

Undeniably, another view on it could justifiably be

For oneself, language isn't needed at all. One understands inner and external environs without use of language. Therefore, linguistic expression which is not comprehended by those for whom it is meant; does not fulfill the most rudimentary & necessary condition of linguistic expression – comprehensibility.

I further analyzed that the longer the gap between thinking and speaking, the higher the possibility of distortion!

Consider a short dialogue: Peter asks, "describe the person, on stairs". Anna replies, "He is a tall, handsome, seemingly Asian man".

In her observational thoughts Anna first categorized him as a man, then analyzed his attributes – tall, handsome, Asian etc. If spoken in concurrence to thought chronology, she should have replied, "He is a man, tall, handsome, seemingly Asian. But linguistic style often violates thought chronology.

Often, quality is comprehended as being a solely comparative assessment. A comparative assessment can be both objective and subjective.

Objective assessment is executed vis-à-vis each/any of the discovered attributes classified into all the four fields, with prescribed or discovered constraints. What are constraints and exclusions has been described ahead in the book.

Subjective assessment of an object or phenomena is done by establishing internal, individual benchmarks of what is ideal, rather than through deductive or inductive analysis.

Quality vis-à-vis description
Former is a subset of latter.

"While description has both categorization and assessment, quality is concerned only with assessment."

In view of the aforementioned, description is used in both cases

- as an output of an investigation as well as
- a specification for design

4.   Concept of Resources

Resource is an **<u>input</u>** or an **<u>output</u>** that is discovered/created and **<u>consumed</u>** **<u>fruitfully</u>** by a **<u>conscious-agent</u>** or **<u>transferred</u>** to another for consumption and is **<u>constrained</u>** in at least one or many of its attributes including supply / availability.

Each of the underlined words have an import and criticality in definition of resource. And below-mentioned is a clear meaning (or say definition) of these constituents that make a resource.

Inputs & outputs

Inputs & outputs factually consist of the same constituents and hence are herein-below clubbed together as one. Constituents of inputs and outputs are:

i.   Information (organized) and modes its transfer through connectivity / network / communication

ii.   Events & Actions, which could either be
(a) Phenomena (occurring by themselves) or
(b) Processes (generated by will and on purpose).
Random events are excluded from inputs and outputs as their fruitfulness cannot be 100% ascertained in advance of them occurring, while fruitfulness is a necessary condition to term anything a resource. Services as an example is an output process that is transferred by the executor to the user.

iii.   Tangibles / Objects

Consumption

An action under which the contributor / creator / generator / executor / owner of an input is also the consumer of the output.

Fruitfulness

Fruitfulness is the concurrence of an input or output to be within **constraints** (quantitative, qualitative, directional, periodicity, positional and possession) that enable fulfilment of a pre-determined purpose. Anything random (object or event) cannot have a pre-determined purpose and hence cannot be categorized as a fruitful resource.

Similarly, anything with no constraints is rarely known to be a resource. While I have never observed anything infinite being a resource, yet I refrain from stating it as a rule, as I allow for such an infinite resource to exist.

Transfer

An action under which the contributor / creator / generator / executor / owner of an input is different from the consumer of the output.

Conscious-Agent

Conscious-agents are best described as viewpoints of two categories of Entities[7]. There are four different conscious-agents:

i. The first conscious-agent(s) is(are) the participating entity (ies) - executor/doer/creator, he (they), without

---

[7] An individual or a group of individuals united in viewpoint or decision: (i) Physical entities incl. a) Individuals, b) Groups & Communities & c) Public-at-large; (ii) Legal entities (Companies, Firms etc.); (iii) Cyber entities (IPs, Domains etc.)

whom the fruitfulness (use) of the resource would have neither been discovered or invented.

ii. The second conscious-agent(s) is(are) the participating entity (ies) - orderer/user/public-at-large, he (they), without whom the fruitfulness (worth/use) of the resource would have never been confirmed.

Both the first & the second conscious-agents generate their own subjective assessments. Subjectivism is critical to be encouraged, as that is what, when generated multiple times from various conscious-agents, leads to an objective understanding of subjective views through statistical evaluation.

iii. The third conscious-agent is that abstract observer, whose viewpoint represents the morality of the society. This agent is expected to know all the true and unmasqueraded views of all the participants therefore, he/she can unmask the intentions behind the creation or user of assessed resource.

iv. The fourth conscious-agent represents the jurist or arbitrator, who knows all the expressed but not unexpressed viewpoints. This conscious-agent tries through deductive reasoning to come to conclusions on what the third conscious-agent would know.

Although there are four conscious-agents, in assessment of microeconomic, the 3rd and 4th conscious-agents are seldom used (but for in circumstances of disputes). Most assessment is limited to the Participating entities (doer / executor /

creator) and Effected entities (orderer / user / public-at-large).

'Constraints' in the context of our book are tolerances (limits) variation within which does not render the resource unfruitful.

Constraints can be in value and/or direction of attributes and have three levels of categorization (types). The first level has two types: Outer and Inner.

LEVEL I: Outer Constraints

These are tolerances (limits) which describe the resistance of the resource from getting declassified as fruitful when exiting the stipulated constraints.

LEVEL I: Inner Constraints

These are minimal upradation levels (hence, inner limits) that are to be achieved barring which the resource will lose its fruitfulness. A good example would be upgrading the Engine's pollution generation norm from Euro V to Euro VI. Once a nation implements it, every such automobile that does not upgrade, will lose its fruitfulness as it will be disallowed to be on roads.

The second Level of Constraint categorization embodies four types of constraints in value & direction – Independent, Unidirectional dependency constraints, Bidirectional dependency constraints, Time-dependent-violation Constraints and Exclusions. We discuss each one of them.

LEVEL II: Independent Constraints

These are tolerances (limits) which are pre-determined & remain unchanged in value and direction notwithstanding the changes in value and direction of other constraints that define fruitfulness of a resource.

Time independent constraints are those that remain unchanged over long foreseeable periods of time (they are not essentially everlasting).

LEVEL II: Unidirectional Dependency Constraints

These are tolerances (limits) which have a pre-determined minimum or a maximum but thereafter the limits are a functional relationship of other constraints defining the various sufficiency attributes of assessed resources.

LEVEL II: Bi-directional Dependency Constraints

These are tolerances (limits) which have neither a pre-determined minimum nor maximum, but are a functional relationship of other constraints defining the various sufficiency attributes of assessed resources.

LEVEL II: Time-dependent-violation Constraints

Not all constraints when violated, render assessed resources fruitless. Some constraint violations are a relationship of violation (units) and the time for which the violation occurred. If the time for which the constraint violation occurred is less than a prescribed value and prescribed time, the resource will not lose its fruitfulness. A good example would be circuits which when undergo a voltage spike for even two times the permissible constraints, but for a picosecond, will not render the circuit useless and damage nothing.

LEVEL II: Exclusions

Exclusions are 'special zones' within the limits and tolerances/constraints specified but an entry to which will render the assessed resource fruitless. Exclusions therefore, never lie beyond the limits prescribed by the constraints. On the contrary they lie within the limits but are islands or zones into which a dynamic resource should not enter or remain in it for a time duration longer than that prescribed (eg: Time-dependent-violation Constraints).

Demonstrating exclusions and constraints:

Imagine defining a straight road –

An area within 3 meters of the straight line joining points 'A' and 'B'. 3 metres from the straight line define the constraint for the road. Now imagine there is a circular embarkment on this road at the first crossing, halfway between 'A' and 'B'. This raised circular embarkment is an exclusion in an otherwise simple constraints within which the road is defined (3m from straight line joining A with B). The circular embarkment is within the limits defining the road, but are excluded from use for apparent reasons.

LEVEL III: Objective Constraints

Objective part of an assessment is that limit which is prescribed a priori – one that is known from existing experiences and observations. Invariably, most attributes are bi-directional and one of the directional limit is objective. The only attributes without any objective constraints are those which have just been discovered or invented. For such attributes, apparently there is no historical record from which to deduce an objective limit. The objective limit is the one that makes the said resource's life-cycle comparable analogues from the same category.

LEVEL III: Subjective Constraints

The other limit is often subjective & established to provide longevity to expensive resources to reduce their cost of ownership over its life cycle. There is no specified limits to subjective constraints.

Following four are the commonest methods for establishing Constraints:

(i)   An ideal, established by inductive logic. Example – "Efficiency is limited to unity";

(ii)   established standards - by law or practice. Example – "Optimal human performance is limited for 8 hours of continuous work";

(iii)   best known or State-of-the-Art exemplar in the said category or field. Example – "40% is the best achieved Gallium Arsenide solar cell efficiency";

(iv) its own state or performance (howsoever defined or accepted by the conscious-agent), previously or prospectively anticipated in future. Example – "The sportsman was performing better 3 years ago".

5. Type of Resources

With clarity on what is a resource, we focus on the types of resources that have been identified by me.

				Quantitative Change in value or direction risk	Qualitative Change in value or direction risk	Geo-Ambient Change in value or direction risk	Possession Change in value or direction risk
1	Elemental	Non-systematic	Micro-Economic or business resources				
2	Elemental	Non-systematic	Socio-Cultural group resources				
3	Elemental	Non-systematic	Emotional resources				
4	Elemental	Non-systematic	Academic-Intellectual behavioural resources				
5	Elemental	Systematic	Politico-legal macro-economic resources				
6	Derivate from [5]	Non-systematic	Administrative & Management resources				
7	Derivate from [4,2,1]	Systematic	Public-health & Existential resources				
8	Derivate from [1,4]	Non-systematic	Technical & Technological resources				
9	Derivate from [1,2]	Non-systematic	Information, Digital & Cyber Access to data resources				
10	Derivate from [1,2,4]	Systematic	Environmental & ambient resources				

'Resources' are of ten types, each listed below.

Each resource can be categorized further into two sub-categories. The first subcategory has two types 'Elemental' and 'Derivate', while the second subcategory has Systematic and Non-Systematic.

The mapping in the table above shows that the latter five resources are derived from a combination of the first five (see from [A,B,C] in the table). Therefore, the first five (Economic, Emotional, Social, Intellectual & politico-legal) are Elemental Resources, while the next bunch of 5 resources (Administrative, Health & Existential, Technical, Informational, Environmental) are Derivate Resources. They are derived from a combination of the Elemental Resources.

Systematic Resources are those which are generated / created / owned not by one person or a small group of them but by large communities, states or nations, collectively. The quality of these resources is generally beyond the control of one or a small group of individual. Systematic resources can neither be generated quickly nor destroyed. Destruction or devaluation of systematic resources impacts entire nations, making even those pay who had not wanted or voted for the change or destruction.

Non-Systematic Resources are those which are generated / created / owned by one person or a small group of them. Non-Systematic resources, if destroyed, impact only the small number of people owning or using these resources.

In the chapter ahead, I have discussed each type of resource identified by me very briefly, so as not to make this book about all the resources. There is an in-depth discussion on Microeconomic Resources which are crucial and embed in themselves a major invention.

5.1. Emotional Resources [Elemental, Non-Systematic]

Emotional resource is the capability of humans to respond to complex situations, where deductive or inductive logic cannot be applied for predicting outcomes. A lack of emotional resources results into human incapability to choose and control emotional responses, particularly to negative situations, without engaging in self-destructive behaviour. Below mentioned are the major (not all) emotional resources:

Self-esteem is having a positive self-worth such that one values his own ideas, actions & abilities.

Self-regulation is the ability to say 'No' to otherwise desired states keeping in mind the impact that continuation of such desired states will have on the future well-being. Avoiding over eating or over consumption of alcohol are instances of such self regulation.

Emotional energy is the capacity to motivate oneself or others in the ambience by positive valence like enthusiasm.

Attachment is the ability to connect emotionally with others.

Resilience is the capability to bounce back and move forward in trying (incl. adverse) circumstances.

Prosilience is the capability to emerge stronger after undergoing adverse circumstances and becoming better than before —.

Agreeableness is the ability to get along well with other people by being warm, friendly, and tactful.

Optimism is the confidence that life will work out, as opposed to the neurotic pattern of excessive worrying.

People are rich in emotional resources if they are high in self-esteem, self-regulation, emotional energy, attachment, resilience, agreeableness, and optimism. As with the other kinds of capital, individuals may vary in the extent to which they have such emotional resources.

What are the origins of emotional resources?

Like other aspects of personality, the causes of emotional resources may be **genetic**, **epigenetic**, **learning**, or **choice**.

Genetic means characteristics such as optimism that are inherited.

Epigenetic means that the genes are turned on or off by chemical modifications that result from environments including while you were in your mother's womb. For example, parents suffering from poor nutrition or stress can produce epigenetic modifications in their offspring.

Learning begins as soon as the brain is sufficiently developed to form new synaptic connections that may influence how new situations are understood and acted on.

Choices are propensities to choose situations like avoiding dangerous people that can have long-term effects on future resources such as emotional energy.

5.2. Socio-cultural Resources [Elemental, Non-Systematic]

Socio-cultural resources are capabilities of an individual to use his background and connections with important and resourceful persons to accomplish his objectives[8] and goals[9]. A theory was presented by Lin in 1982 on *the social resources hypothesis*, the *strength-of-position hypothesis*, and the *strength-of-ties hypothesis*. There is substantial literature available on Socio-cultural resources, and I have very little to add to it of my own.

To learn in-depth about two vital sub-categorizes that account for 80% of what is valuable in Socio-Cultural Resources – Influence and Power, I propose reader to study my Book 'Living – Vol 3, Influence and Power'. It is available on Amazon/Kindle in both paperback and as an eBook (ISBN: 9798604179987; ASIN: B0846LVF75). The book in a brief text of less than 80 pages, provides intellectually dense content that enables understanding of what are socio-cultural resources and why they are.

5.3. Academic-scientific-intellectual Resources [Elemental, Non-Systematic]

These are informational resources encompassing exclusive knowledge that can be used to either enhance social systems like education or defence or business.

---

[8] Objectives are milestones to achieve larger goals. Objectives are usually quantitative.

[9] Goals are long term goals that are could be directional rather than being specific destinations.

5.4. Political & legal Resources [Elemental, Systematic]

These are resources that procure accomplishment of objectives and goals through use of ideologically connected humans. Knowledge of legal processes to achieve one's goals is a major resource.

5.5. Administrative Resources [Derivate, Non-systematic]

Administrative resources are capabilities to procure accomplishment of works through use of administrative authority.

5.6. Public-health & Existential Resources [Derivate, Systematic]

Public health resource is the capability to procure healthcare services including diagnosis, treatment and holistic cure such that sustainability & survivability are ensured. This also includes the capability to defend oneself or one's society from internal or external aggression.

5.7. Technical & Technological Resources [Derivate, Non-systematic]

Technical resources are capabilities to create and maintain technical equipment that enable mechanization, digitization and automation of various production processes. Technological on the other hand pertain to availability of knowledge to execute complex technical tasks repeatedly without digressions.

5.8. Information, Digital & Cyber Access Resources [Derivate, Non-systematic]

Information resource is capability to acquire, possess and use information including but not limited to technical fields that enable procurement of various

This is the capability to exploit Environment, if needed, but causing pollution, without substantially deteriorating the environmental and ambient conditions.

I have circumvented writing beyond identifying resources, barring Microeconomic resources on which there is a major body of innovative work done by me. Hence, on Microeconomics Resource section is the focus attempted in sections ahead. If at all there will be something innovative and important to add in the list of all other resources (barring Microeconomics) I shall do it in the next editions of this book.

5.10. Microeconomic Resources [Elemental, Non-systematic]

In a stable & good political environment / ambience economic resources are the most basic resources which are a currency for procuring and consuming all other resources. But in an unstable or bad political environment / ambience, economic resources are derived from Political & Administrative resources (in future it could be technical resources) – hence corruption.

Microeconomic Resources are further subdivided into four kinds along with 3rd level divisions of each subdivision.

			Quantitative Change in value or direction	Qualitative Change in value or direction	Geo-Ambient Change in value or	Possession Change in value or direction
1.1	Primary	Attention				
1.2		Time				
1.3	Secondary	Skills				
1.4		Space				

1.5	Tertiary	Manpower				
1.6		Machine				
1.7		Service				
1.8		Process				
1.9		Premise				
1.10	Transactional	Monetary				
1.11		Material				

Therefore, "accomplishment of targeted outputs with least investment of resources" means investment of any type of resources that includes the first eight and all their subdivisions. It therefore, includes attention and time of people of microeconomic entity.

Definition of Microeconomic Resources

From 3rd Chapter it has been discovered that assessment has four fields.

Resources are inputs (/outputs), availability (/supply) of which is constrained.

A priori, constraints can be spotted only in that, which can be assessed. That which cannot be assessed, cannot be constrained. Therefore, using the understanding of Fields of assessment, I concluded to detail the aforementioned definition of resources:

Resources are anything availability/supply of which is constrained by – (i) ownership[10], (ii) quantitative attributes, (iii) qualitative attributes, (iv) Geo-ambience[11].

I am giving below unconventional examples of resources, constrained by one of the four aforementioned. Imagine anything and the given definition will enable you to distinguish a resource from non-resources. Anything tangible or intangible, active or inactive, dead or alive; only if constrained in one of these four categories enables it to be treated as Microeconomic Resource (this concept will be relevant in the Chapter 'Definition of Quality').

(a) Quantitative Constraints (Dimensions, Size, Numbers, Volume): A modeling Co. needs people of specific girth, who are not infinitely available, making such people an economic resource, while the rest like me are not. Quantitative constraints could be in value or direction.

(b) Qualitative Constraints (Properties): Clean rooms require clean air. Clean air is obtained by filtering ambient air, making it an economic resource, while ambient air is not one. Qualitative constraints could be in value or direction.

(c) Geo-Ambience (Location): Water from a spring is freely available at the springs, but when available in a bottle on the tabletop, it becomes a microeconomic resource. Therefore, same water in nature is not a microeconomic resource, but on the table-top it is.

---

[10] As defined in Chapter 3, 'Ownership' in context of this book is stands for the observer, user, orderer, participant and impact bearers of change - the conscious-agent, on whose behalf parameters for other three fields are set, who is foremost impacted by change in the attributes of the assessed resource and a change in whom leads to changes in assessed attributes of all other fields

[11]Physical location and environs in which contained.

(d) Ownership: A river has a spontaneous existence, but the moment a nation claims its rights over its waters, it becomes an economic resource and a matter of give & take between countries & states through which a single river flows.

Primary Microeconomic Resources

There are two Primary Resources– (a) **TIME** & (b) **ATTENTION**. While 'Time' is easy to understand, 'Attention' is little twisty. 'Attention' in our context means the ability of people to focus themselves on something to make it happen, evidently using their own mental and physical strength; as also the ability to getting others focus on something to make it happen, evidently using others' mental and physical strength. 'Time' is constrained in quantity & location & ownership. While 'Attention' is constrained in quantity & properties.

(i) Attention =

[Minimum of (either Actual input time; or Standard input time established by experience or a third party; or the minimum input time ever consumed for achieving similar output)]

[divided by]

[Time input in man-hours to achieve a desired output]

'ATTENTION' can therefore, never be more than unity. While minimum of three cases ensures that, the best case with highest focus is the benchmark.

'TIME' on the other hand, to be a resource, has also to be rated vis-à-vis some output or activity or else it is of little use and hence not a resource. To induce an understanding of 'TIME' as a resource, consider it as duration that is invested by an individual or a group to achieve specific outputs. Therefore, 'TIME' becomes a resource only when entities utilize their working capacity to achieve certain outputs/goals. Alternatively said, 'TIME' as a resource is capacity.

Capacity of an individual or a team to achieve specific outputs =

No. of input man hours

[divided by]

[No. of people used x 24 x No. of calendar days used]

Capacity (Time) too is never more than unity.

It is logically deducible that Capacity times of Attention is the Capability that an entity has.

Capability of an individual or a team = Attention x Capacity

Since both attention and capacity are below unity by definition, so is capability. Generally, capability of an entity (individual or a group) does not change in short span of time, therefore, attention & capacity are mutually compensating – higher focus needs lesser time to provide an output, while lesser focus needs more time for the same output; something we know from common sense. This becomes potent and even critical in evaluating people.

Though it is possible to scientifically arrive at absolute value of 'Attention' as 'fruitful time ÷ Total input Time', (whereby fruitful-time is the time spend on thinking or acting for achievement of desired output, while adding the time of distraction to it will give the total input time), as technology today might enable to do this by brain mapping. Nonetheless, this might be academically useful, in day-to-day activity it is easier to go with a comparative definition, as expressed above in (i).

Common sense shows that it is not suitable to assess 'Attention' absolutely. It is better assessed comparatively in possible three cases – Mr. A's attention span vis-à-vis Mr. B's or Mr. A's attention span yesterday vis-à-vis today or Mr. A's attention span vis-à-vis the highest Attention span recorded till date [all three cases are captured in (i)].

Alternatively said, the Capability of an entity (individual or a group) to achieve specific outputs is the primary resource and is a product of the two primary resources - 'Attention' & 'Time'. By quantifying 'Attention' & 'Time' & in consequence 'Capacity' & relating it to human beings & teams, I laid the foundations of a completely Automated Evaluation & Assessment System that I described in full in my book 'Transformers' (ISBN: 978-1514861240, ASIN: B07Y6QZS42).

Secondary Microeconomic Resources
Secondary resources are two and are generated by amalgamation of the primary resources.

(i)   KNOWLEDGE/SKILLS : Constrained in quantity, properties, ownership and location

(ii) SPACE : Constrained in quantity, properties, ownership and location
      Secondary resources are formed by variously combining Primary Resources. Time and Attention together make skills & knowledge happen. Space is also created by human time and attention – whether it is a building or it is a field with crops.

Tertiary Microeconomic Resources

Tertiary resources are formed by combining primary and secondary resources and are:

(i)   MANPOWER : Man-owned skills combined with knowledge he possesses for introducing or reproducing processes. This resource is usually constrained in quantity, properties, and location;

(ii)   MACHINE : Human skills algorithmized for reproducing actions and processes by equipment and till 20th century even by animals. This resource is usually constrained in quantity, properties, ownership;

(iii) SERVICES : Skills unavailable internally and hired from an external party. This resource is usually constrained in quantity, properties, and ownership;

(iv)   PREMISES (LAND/BUILDING) : Formed by skills applied to space. This resource is constrained in quantity, properties, ownership and location;

(v)   PROCESSES : Standard methods of achieving certain results, using knowledge & skills. This resource is constrained in properties and ownership.

Transactional Microeconomic Resources

These are two (i) MATERIALS / ENERGY / UTILITIES; (ii) CAPITAL. They are constrained in quantity, ownership, & properties. They keep on constantly transforming, from one form to other, from converging and diverging in various combinations from Primary to Secondary to Tertiary Resources. TRANSACTIONAL RESOURCES are the currency, medium and denomination of all the difference types & transformations of Resources. Transactional Resources also do cross-transformations – that is Material to Capital & vice-versa.

Materials & Energy are both - the basic input as well as the final output. Indeed, all socio-economics is the process of transformation of one material into another or into capital. This is the reason I term these Resources Transactional. All transformations in Transactional Resources are catalyzed by Tertiary Resources.

Conclusively, the two basic resources we have are 'Time' & 'Attention' (we may refer them collectively as 'Capability'). We know most of the aforementioned instinctively or by common sense. I have articulated it by creating a framework. Don't we say to our children, "pay attention as higher attention will save you time and in the saved time you make Lego homes"? Indeed, upon a break-down to motives, one will conclude that all that we do is one of following three (other than idling) – (i) either gaining skills and knowledge; or (ii) creating / transforming space; or (iii) transacting / creating / transforming transactional resources including their cross-transformations.

Declassification of resources as unfruitful

A resource is considered declassified from being fruitful when it fails to fulfill the sufficiency conditions, which so ever are established by an organization, community, nation, government or department.

Declassification of Primary Resources (Attention & Capacity)

Declassification of someone's attention span as an unfruitful resource can be done by establishing the average or median levels of Attention (as defined in the previous section on Primary Resources) in an organization and then comparative to it establish the threshold below which Attention of an employee or participant of the organization be considered unfruitful. Similarly, organizations can establish thresholds for Capacity below which Capacity of the participant will be considered as an unfruitful resource.

Declassification of Secondary Resources (Space & Skills)

Any change in the space available to an organization below or above a specific threshold can be declassified as a fruitful resource.

Skills in many sectors are often needed to be upgraded (pilots, doctors etc.). If these skills aren't updated, the skills, as they exist in professionals have a tendency to be declassified as fruitful resources. It is important to note that this is most neglected aspect of description, quality and assessment.

Declassification of Tertiary Resources (Manpower, Machine, Services, Premises and Processes)

Declassification of tertiary resources is to be established by every organization on its own depending on the minimally acceptable levels of performance of any of the aforementioned resources.

Declassification of Transactional Resources (Materials/Energy/Utilities and Money)

Materials are declassified, if they fail to meet necessary or sufficiency conditions established.

Energy and utilities are considered declassified for similar conditions – gas with low power cannot be used for power production. Power supplied at very low voltage is equally useless.

Money is the only resource that is never declassified as a resource but for the Government to do it for sovereign reasons.

6.   Necessary Attributes' Framework - Safety First

Safety attributes includes the safety of the Inputs-&-Outputs[12], the ambience-&-environs and humans through the process of generation/creation, storage & use of the same.

Safety is driven by two of its constituents:

(a) Identification of all major known[13] risks and creation of a mitigation strategy in advance.

(b) Having in place, a clear plan/understanding on who will address the uncertainties that arise and how.

Zero-day-risk[14] is called an uncertainty.

Quantifiably, risk is assessed by considering historical behaviors and outcomes and ideally constantly running algorithms for the probability of a risk case occurring in a feedback loop. For lack of having occurred / recorded / comprehended before, uncertainties are incalculable.

---

[12] Inputs & outputs consist of same constituents and are therefore clubbed together. Constituents of inputs and outputs are (i) Information (organized) and modes of its transfer; (ii) Events & Actions, which could either be (a) Phenomena (occurring by themselves) or (b) Processes (generated by will and on purpose). Fruitfulness is a necessary condition to term anything a resource. Services as an example is an output process that is transferred by the executor to the user; (iii) Tangibles / Objects.

[13] 'Known' here means known to mankind and not known to oneself. Therefore, discovering this known needs research and should be handled by experts who have exceled in understanding elements of risk.

[14] A risk which has no history of appearance and hence has happened for the first time. The analogy is drawn from Zero Day Cyber Attack – one which is a new kind and has not recorded history or analogues available in maleware libraries.

Definition of Risk

Pertaining to inputs-&-outputs (resources) of all kind, risk unambiguously is "the probability of disqualification of resources as fruitful".

Hence, risks are classified in terms of classification of resources.

Risk and passage of time

Risks and time passage have a foundational relationship. At the time of acquisition or generation of a resource, there is no risk calculable or possible. When a resource has risen (created or procured) it can only be qualified as either fit or unfit. If it is unfit, it has to be discarded. In case it is fit[15] and in consequence - acquired (or created, or made functional), risks arise in the period that follows such procurement (generation) of the resource. Along with functionalization of resources, post-assessment of their fitness, risks and sufficiency attributes (or conditions) kick in.

This relationship of Risk and passage of time is indeed defined as the probability of an input/output being rendered fruitless (declassified as fruitful resource) with passage of time owing to it violating the constraints laid down for its fruitfulness.

Therefore, risks & uncertainties both are classified akin to classification of resources. This implies there are ten different types of risks in concurrence to ten type of resources.

---

[15] for the purpose it is done, the time at which it happened, geo-ambience at/in which it happened and the cost at which it is acquired/created.

SN	Elemental (E) / Derivate (D)	Systematic (S) / Non-Systematic (N)	RISK CATEGORIES	FIELDS OF ASSESSMENT			
				Quantitative Change in value or direction risk	Qualitative Change in value or direction risk	Geo-Ambient Change in value or direction risk	Possession Change in value or direction risk
1	E	N	Microeconomic or business risks				
2	E	N	Socio-Cultural group risks				
3	E	N	Emotional risks				
4	E	N	Academic-Intellectual-Scientific behavioural risks				
5	D	N	Administrative & Management Risks				
6	E	S	Politico-legal, macro-economic risks				
7	D from [4,2,1]	S	Public-health & existential risks				
8	D from [1,4]	N	Technical & Technological risks				
9	D from [1,2]	N	Information, Digital & Cyber Access to data risks				
10	D from [1,2,4]	S	Environmental and Ambient risks				

Microeconomic (/Business) Risks:

			Quantitative Change in value or direction risk	Qualitative Change in value or direction risk	Geo-Ambient Change in value or direction risk	Possession Change in value or direction risk
1.1	Primary Business Risks	Risk of lack of Attention				
1.2		Risk of lack of Time				
1.3	Secondary Business Risks	Risk of lack of Skills				
1.4		Risk of lack of Space				
1.5	Tertiary Business Risks	Manpower associated Risks				
1.6		Machine failure associated risks				
1.7		Service quality failure risks				
1.8		Process failure				
1.9		Premise inadequacy risks				
1.10	Transactional Business Risks	Monetary Financial Risks				
1.11		Material Risks				

Aforementioned risk categories are critical for the process of risk identification because they act as horizontal guides to channel deep vertical thinking on what all risks in each category exist.

It is worth mentioning that within each of the aforementioned categories and sub-categories there are further divisions and categorizations. A good example would be at least 15 types of financial (monetary) risks that are known.

My critical inventions are the understanding that risks are probabilities of some resource being rendered unfruitful. And hence the primary category of risks is akin to category of resources.

Further divisions of these two level risks (10 Resource Type Risks including Microeconomic Risks which are further divided into 11 microeconomic / business risk types) are known and there is little to add to existing literature.

Similarly, methods and processes of calculating these risks and setting the acceptable levels as part of necessary attributes too is well known and do not merit my intervention as there is nothing very novel that I have to offer on probability calculations, which are known to any school boy or a science graduate today.

Since risk is a probability, it does not usually have a simple binary state. Therefore, a binary state is forced by mentioning the minimum or maximum limits to acceptable risk probability levels; along with sometimes, in rare cases – rate of growth of risk. Rate of growth is important because, there are multiple such operations, where it is not possible to abort an action instantaneously. Any such aborting, actually leads to first lessening of the pace and subsequent seizure. Epidemics is a good example. In case any Government decides to impose a quarantine-curfew, forcing people to stay at home to avoid spread of infection and target to limit the infected patients in the country to 1000. It is important to establish when to impose the curfew so that the total number does not exceed 1000, come what may. This is done by understanding the rate of growth. Apparently, in case of epidemic, the Government will have to press the paddle on complete seizure of activities and imposition of curfew the moment number of infected patients crosses 600 (arbitrary number, it could be any other depending on the rate of growth) because there is a pace of deceleration at which the infection reduces. It does not cease to be transmitted instantaneously.

Binary state imposition is necessary because that is the nature of necessary attributes. They have to be in the form of a go/no-go checklist, to ascertain the fulfillment or non-fulfillment of conditions.

It's like the aeroplane checklist and flight checklist. Latter is all about necessary conditions, the check is done just before the flight leaves the tarmac. If any of the checkboxes are not ticked, the flight is not released. Aeroplane checklists are Sufficiency Attributes, these are done after a few flights to check what are the changes that have happened in the plane, through its use and what all needs to be measured or changed as per instructions.

7. Emotional Connect Framework

Emotional connect is a purely subjective assessment of a resource by the conscious-agent such that the agent needs no reason or justification of having or not having an emotional connect.

There are two types of subjective Emotional Connect Assessments of the resource in question.

Emotional Connect Assessments

(i)   Absolute Emotional Connect – it is binary (Yes/No)

(ii) Comparative Emotional Connect – Also binary (Y/N)

Assessing Conscious-Agents

There are two conscious-agents, whose emotional connect is important to be established in hurdle-rank[16] for assessment of the resource being evaluated. First conscious-agent to evaluate and clear the resource is the Participating Entity (doer/executor/creator) of the resource. Second conscious-agent to evaluate the resource is the Effected entity (orderer/validator/approver) of the resource.

Emotional Connect is a deep subject, discussed and described in my Book 'Likeability'. I strongly recommend it (though in advance of its publication) to those interested in fathoming the phenomena of emotional connect. For the purpose of this

---

[16] Hurdle-Rank in the context of our Book, means affirmative emotional connect of the first in sequence (Doer/creator) is essential to consider the response on emotional connect of the second (orderer/user) in order. If the first in hurdle-rank assesses lack of emotional connect, the second is not even asked for. Therefore, in hurdle-ranking, assessment terminates the moment a negative review is received, while the resource is assessed to have been assessed as previous hurdle compliant.

book, we consider expression of emotional connect framework in four fields, all binary & sequential. There are no constraints in this framework of assessment

Fields of the Absolute Emotional Connect

(i) Does the Participating Entity (doer/maker) feel an emotional connect with the resource assessed or not? Assessment is completely subjective & binary, that is - confirmation or negation.

(ii) Does the Effected Entity (orderer/user(s)/public-at-large) feel an emotional connect with the resource assessed or not? Assessment is completely subjective & binary, that is - confirmation or negation.

Fields of the Comparative Emotional Connect

(i) Has the Participating Entity (doer/maker) concluded that the resource under assessment is best of all experienced or known (par excellence for doer) him till date? The choice is binary – is the assessed resource best or not?

(ii) Has the Effected Entity (orderer/user(s)/public-at-large) concluded that the resource under assessment is best of all experienced or known (par excellence for orderer/user)? The choice is binary – is the assessed resource best or not?

For the purposes of this Book, each aforementioned field of Emotional Connect exists in Yes/No binary.

Emotional connect (likeability) in general context has been invented and patented by the author, so kindly await publication, which will be made available on http://www.deepakloomba.in/books/

8.   Aesthetic Framework

Aesthetic Framework has two fields and is ternary[17]. That is – either something is aesthetic or not. This is so because of how we define Aesthetic Value.

Definition of Absolute Aesthetic Value

Absolute Aesthetic is that which possesses universal absolute emotional connect (likeability). 'Universal' stands for roaring majority and is an arbitrary percentage (Value) of those confirming an absolute emotional connect, of the total interviewed.

Definition of Comparative Aesthetic Value

Comparative Aesthetic is that which possesses universal comparative emotional connect (likeability). 'Universal' stands for roaring majority and is an arbitrary percentage (Value) of those confirming a comparative-emotional-connect[18], of the total interviewed.

A comparatively aesthetic resource is better than Absolutely aesthetic as it is rated not just likeable by most, but is rated the best by them among the analogues. Making it Aesthetic and Par Excellent simultaneously.

It is interesting that emotional connect (likeability) is completely subjective. But universal emotional connect (likeability) is objective. The rationale behind such conclusion is uncomplicated. If most ('most' is arbitrarily

---

[17] That which assumes three values

[18] Comparative emotional connect stands for a declaration by the effected entity that the emotional connect (likeability) felt with assessed resource is best when compared all analogues experience till date. One can term it 'Par Excellence'.

defined) of those interviewed on their emotional connect with the assessed resource affirm, the assessed resource can be claimed to be liked by all. The likeability of the assessed resource in such case becomes objective, since it is valid for all.

It is important to remind the reader that we had in the context of this book defined 'objectivity' to be that which is quantitatively &/or qualitatively affirmed similarly by everyone experiencing it & remains unchanged on repeated assessments within a reasonable timeframe.

As is apparent from aforementioned, there are two issues that need to be dealt with to establish Aesthetic Value of a resource.

Firstly, a sensible size vote with ternary choice is mandatory – (i) Vote percentage of those who confirm an emotional connect, of the total interviewed; (ii) Yes (it is aesthetic, if the vote exceeds the stipulated constraint); (iii) No (it is not aesthetic, if the vote doesn't exceed the stipulated constraint). In view of aforementioned, a number of people need to be interviewed physically by a surveyor or electronically/online, to acquire the view of the participating and effected parties (latter are more important and include orderers, users, public-at-large) on the emotional connect they feel with the resource assessed. Only a roaring majority (universal) vote confirming emotional connect makes the assessed resource Aesthetic. 'Aesthetic', otherwise is neither universally defined, nor accepted. Aesthetic value is therefore statistical in nature and can only be claimed after gathering enough 'likeness' data from various popular evaluations.

Secondly, an arbitrary but reasonable, dynamic percentage needs to be ascertained (which should ideally alter with total orderer/user(s) surveyed) on affirmation of which, of presence of emotional connect, can the assessed or evaluated resource be declared aesthetic.

It is difficult to create a static percentage, because roaring majority or universal likeability can be declared on affirmation of emotional connect to the resource of nine out of ten cases surveyed. But ninety out of hundred is not adequate. For universal emotional connect, one would ideally desire an affirmation of may be ninety five out of hundred. Similarly, in 1000 cases one would expect 980 affirmations to term the resource aesthetic. Candidly, there is no specific rule for percentage of affirmations to establish a resource to be aesthetic. But one thing is for sure - the percentage of affirmations needed will keep on rising with the total number of cases. Underlying logic is in sync with Borel's law of large numbers that postulates that as the number of cases increase, the empirical probability tends more and more to theoretical one. In other words – on tossing a coin 10 times there is a possibility of getting all ten heads. But on tossing 1 million times (case B) it is impossible to get 1 million heads, the results will be closer to 500,000 for each (head & tail), the distribution in case of 10 million cases (case C) will be further closer to 50-50 probability when compared to Case B. Thus, it is but natural to expect that to term something universally emotionally connected to; the universality in percentage has to keep on increasing with increase in number of cases surveyed.

9.   Description and its elements

Conclusively, description of all resources (inputs/outputs) - tangible & intangible (including but not limited to events, objects, processes or phenomena) that are constrained in supply or availability, is established by evaluating it in four frameworks and associated fields thereby assessing the values and directions of the attributes belonging to the fields of each of the framework.

(A) Necessary Attributes' Framework

(A.1.) Safety First

Safety of the Inputs-&-Outputs[19], the ambience-&-environs and humans through the process of generation/creation, storage & use of the same.

Safety is driven by two of its constituents:

(i) Assessment of risks (probability of occurrence of an adverse event) along with establishment of the maximum and/or minimum requirements (as applicable) of the risk levels (quantifiable) along with identification of the acceptable rates of growth and/or decline.

(ii) Having in place, a clear understanding and plan on who/how will damages arising from uncertainties be assessed & mitigated.

Risks are categorized akin to resource categories.

---

[19] Inputs & outputs consist of same constituents and are therefore clubbed together. Constituents of inputs and outputs are (i) Information (organized) and modes of its transfer; (ii) Events & Actions, which could either be (a) Phenomena (occurring by themselves) or (b) Processes (generated by will and on purpose). Fruitfulness is a necessary condition to term anything a resource. Services as an example is an output process that is transferred by the executor to the user; (iii) Tangibles / Objects.

(A.2.) Fitness attributes

Stands for suitability (or in rare cases mandatory unsuitability) of the resources to the conditions prescribed for Fitness attributes in the fields of (1) purpose, (2) time, (3) geoambience and (4) cost as established by the owner/creator of the resource.

Fitness attributes are binary. Therefore, the value of the fitness attribute is either fit (surpasses the hurdle value) or unfit.

Fitness Fields only have values, but no direction. As Fitness is assessed only once while the resource is generated or procured. Changes are monitored only in Sufficiency Attributes. And therefore, the Fields of Sufficiency Attributes' Framework have both values and directions.

(B) Sufficiency Attributes' Framework

Sufficiency conditions are considered accomplished, if

(B.1.) the assessed resource has good/high (in rare cases – absence) resistance to weathering & remaining qualified as a useful resource XXX (fruitful resource is discussed further in detail, in next chapter) for good time.

(B.2.) the assessed resource is upgraded (changed) regularly to ensure that it does not become obsolete by virtue of termination of its market life rather than its technical or material life.

Constraints in both the aforementioned cases (B.1. & B.2.) are established and assessment done by monitoring changing values and directions of the attributes constituting each of the four fields of Framework – (Ownership, Quantitative, Qualitative, Geo-Ambience).

Sufficiency Attributes of assessed resources in all four fields are monitored for changes in their values & directions to ascertain that deviations if at all are within the constraints; through the period of utilization of resource. Such that the fruitfulness of the resource is maintained. Changes are monitored only in Sufficiency Attributes Framework, as in the other three frameworks only spot values at the time of assessment are considerd.

(C) Emotional Connect Attributes' Framework

(C.1.) Ascertain whether Conscious-agent(s) (doer / maker) feels an emotional connect with the assessed resource. The choice of the conscious-agent is 100% subjective and is binary, that is - assessed resource is either liked or not liked.

(C.2.) Ascertain whether Conscious-agent(s) (doer / maker) feels that when compared with his past experiences with resources of same class (and hence, up-front classification is vital) is the current resource best experienced till date? Par Excellence for doer?

(C.3.) Ascertain whether Conscious-agent(s) (orderer / user(s)) feels an emotional connect with the assessed resource. The choice of the conscious-agent is 100% subjective and is binary, that is - assessed resource is either liked or not liked.

(C.4.)   Ascertain whether Conscious-agent (orderer / user(s)) feels that when compared with his past experiences with resources of same class (and hence, up-front classification is vital) is the current resource best experienced till date? Par Excellence for orderer?

All the above-mentioned four Fields of Emotional Connect Framework have only Values (no directions), which are binary, that is – either there is an emotional connect or there is none.

Another important statistical output that can be deduced is by plotting repeated confirmations of absolute or comparative emotional connects of the total number of re-experiences (from categories).

Emotional connect (likeability) in general context has been invented and patented by the author, so please await publication of the patent, which I will make available on my website http://www.deepakloomba.in as well as my blog https://www.chinggary.blogspot.com.

(D) Aesthetic Attributes' Framework

This Framework has two fields:

(D.1.)   Absolute Aesthetics: This field is ternary. It can take three possible values – yes / no / value. 'Value' here stands for the percentage of interviewees, who confirm Absolute Emotional Connect with the resource vis-à-vis total interviewed.

Therefore,

**Absolute Aesthetic Value is =
Affirmed Absolute Emotional Connect**

$\div$

Total No. of surveys.

In case the absolute aesthetic value is close to unity, the resource can be termed Absolutely Aesthetic. The more are the number of cases, the closer is the absolute aesthetic value required to be to unity.

(D.2.) Comparative Aesthetics: This field is ternary. It can take three possible values – yes / no / value. 'Value' stands for the percentage of interviewees, who confirm Comparative Emotional Connect with the resource vis-à-vis total interviewed.

Therefore,

**Comparative Aesthetic Value is =
Affirmed Comparative Emotional Connect**

$\div$

Total No. of surveys.

In case the Comparative aesthetic value is close to unity, the resource can be termed Comparatively Aesthetic. The more are the number of cases, the closer is the absolute aesthetic value required to be to unity.

There is another interesting aspect of Aesthetics which can be probed through repeated voting – Change in Aesthetic Value. This occurs by two means – (i) by plotting the Absolute Aesthetic Values vs time; (ii) by plotting comparative Aesthetic Values vs time.

Hurdle-Ranking

One of the most critical aspects of DNSEA description is hurdle-ranking, which means that there is a pre-determined sequence in the process of description of a resource. The hurdle-rank of assessment is the highest such Framework-Field-Value(/Direction) that is affirmative such that all values preceding are also affirmative. Therefore, in case a resource is safe, meets all fitness conditions, is sufficiently stable in ownership but is not quantitatively sufficient; then in such case evaluation ends at the first negative assessment. The resource is assessed as 'sufficiently good for ownership'. Even if it is good-looking, emotional connect is ignored. Therefore, in DNSEA description, each field of each framework is a hurdle, which if unsurpassed, leads to ceasing of assessment there itself and its ranking at the last affirmative field.

An ideal Resource (goods or services)

This understanding that complete description can be provided when necessary, sufficiency, emotional & aesthetic attributes of an object are described, owes its origin to the realization that any resource suitable or ideal has to be

(i)   Safe with low probability of being declassified as a resource;

(ii)   fulfilling the purpose at the time when it is required, in the place or ambience it is required and within a cost which is affordable;

(iii)   should have a long technical & material life-cycle by being a useful resource for long and hence have a low life-cycle cost;

(iv)   ideally, should be functionally upgradable;
(v)   has to be liked by the doer / maker first & orderer /
        user next;
(vi)   ideally, it should be statistically liked by almost all in
        a specific category of people or by public-at-large.

While the concept of safety (identification of risks and their mitigation) & fitness-for-purpose are easy to understand, sufficiency attributes require comprehension, as they are linked closely to my unified theory of resources. Understanding resource & its life-cycle is critical for establishment of sufficiency. Sufficiency attributes of description are those that describe the resistivity of inputs or outputs [both explained ahead] to declassification as a fruitful resource.

Similarly, safety is also derived from the risk (probability) of the resources being declassified as fruitful.

10. Sufficiency Attribute's Framework & Conditions for DNSEA

Sufficiency attributes & conditions in the concept of **DNSEA** are those that define two aspects each with four fields:

(a) the resistance of an input/output (Resource) to weathering & consumption leading to a real or forecasted declassification (as fruitless) of the resource constrained in four fields mentioned in (c).

Change is resisted in all the above fields of the Sufficiency Framework. Any change beyond an established constraint (see page 34 Constraints) declassifies the resource from being fruitful.

The constraints describing resistance of a resource are termed outer constraints.

(b) incapability/failure to upgrade constraints and attributes, as also build newer attributes in concurrence to (i) the market trends and (ii) new knowledge; to avoid declassification of the resource owing to end of its market life before technical.

Change is essential in these cases. Non-accomplishment of a prescribed change declassifies the resource from being a fruitful one.

(c) Four fields in which this framework's attributes and concurrence with relevant constraints and exclusions are:

(i)   Quantitative – Quantitative constraints in value and/or direction of the assessed resource;

(ii)   Qualitative – Qualitative constraints in value &/or direction of properties (physical, chemical, nuclear, mechanical, electrical, magnetic, electromagnetic, optical, biological, biophysical etc.) of the resource assessed;

(iii)   Geo-ambient – Geo-ambient constraints in value and/or direction of the physical, spatial location and the environs &/or ambience in which the assessed resource is contained;

(iv)   Ownership - Ownership constraints are the limitations on who all can be the conscious-agents assessing the resource and includes - the (a) participating parties [creator(s) / doer(s)], (ii) effected parties [the orderer(s) / user(s)].

Constraints & Exclusions - Resistivity to declassification as resource

Comparative assessment can be both objective and subjective. Objective constraint of an attribute for a field of assessment is prescribed a priori – one that is known from existing experiences and observations. Invariably, most attributes are bi-directional and one of the directional limit is objective. The objective limit is the one that makes the said resource valid in its life to analogues from same category.

In a previous chapter we defined four common methods for establishment of constraints:

(i)   An ideal, established by inductive logic. Example –
        "Efficiency is limited to unity";

(ii)   established standards - by law or practice. Example –
        "Optimal human performance is limited for 8 hours of
        continuous work";

(iii)   best known or State-of-the-Art exemplar in the said
        category or field. Example – "40% is the best
        achieved Gallium Arsenide solar cell efficiency";

(iv)   its own state or performance (howsoever defined or
        accepted by the conscious-agent), previously or
        prospectively anticipated in future. Example – "The
        sportsman was performing better 3 years ago".

For describing sufficiency attributes therefore, both the classes of sufficiency with four types constraints exhibit the resistivity of the object-of-assessment to its declassification as a useful resource are to be established. This can be accomplished by establishing the **constraints** and **exclusions** by asking oneself –

Establishing Constraints & Exclusions
Which are the valid constraints to the attribute of a frame's field?

To do the same use a checklist:

ATTRIBUTE NAME	
LEVEL I	
☐ Outer Constraints	☐ Inner Constraints
LEVEL II	

☐ Independent Constraints	☐ Unidirectional Dependency Constraints	☐ Bi-directional Dependency Constraints	☐ Time-dependent-violation Constraints	☐ Exclusions
LEVEL III				
☐ Objective Constraints			☐ Subjective Constraints	

A. OWNERSHIP CONSTRAINTS

A LEVEL I Outer Constraints: Does the thing under consideration undergo change in ownership – that is are the Participating or Effected Conscious-Agents are changing with time? If yes, what kind of ownership change is acceptable? Which of the limits (minimum or maximum or both) to change are mandatory (either or both) by – (i) theory or (ii) law & established standards, or (iii) best local/global practices, making such mandatory limit objective, as it will be applicable on all. All other limits to changes, which are posed internally or individually and are not mandated are completely subjective. Does the thing in question possess this specification, if yes, what is it?

A LEVEL I Inner Constraints: Does the resource under consideration need an ownership change essentially to remain a fruitful resource in market.

A LEVEL II Constraints: Decide relevant applicable constraints for the attribute assessed. Decide whether applicable LEVEL II constraints are – (i) Independent Constraints, (ii) Unidirectional Dependency Constraints, (iii) Bi-directional Dependency Constraints; (iv) Time-dependent-violation Constraints; (v) Exclusions.

A LEVEL II Exclusions: Does the resource under consideration have islands of ownership exclusions – such conscious agents who are not permitted to create or use the said resource, which if not earmarked, could render the resource fruitless or indeed dangerous. A good example would be mentioning on the Pharmaceutical or health drinks - the warning for pregnant women to avoid consuming them for safeguarding.

A LEVEL III Objective Constraints: Decide which of the ownership constraints are objective. Usually in (minimally) bi-directional constraints, one is objective barring those attributes, which are completely new global discoveries or inventions.

A LEVEL III Subjective Constraints: Decide which of the ownership constraints are subjective. Usually in (minimally) bi-directional constraints, one is subjective. The subjective one decides the life-cycle cost of ownership.

B. QUANTITATIVE CONSTRAINTS

B LEVEL I Outer Constraints: Does the thing under consideration undergo change in quantity or dimensions with time? If yes, is it permissible? If permissible, by what value or quantity is it acceptable? Which of the limits (minimum or maximum or both) to change are mandatory (either or both) by – (i) theory or (ii) law & established standards, or (iii) best local/global practices, making such mandatory limit objective, as it will be applicable on all. All other limits to changes, which are posed internally or individually and are not mandated are completely subjective. Does the resource in question possess this specification? If no, elaborate.

B LEVEL I Inner Constraints: Does the thing under consideration need a quantitative upgrade to remain a fruitful resource in market. Upgrade is defined as betterment (as betterment may be described) of parameters that have been defined in constraints.

B LEVEL II Constraints: Decide relevant applicable constraints for the attribute assessed. Decide whether applicable LEVEL II constraints are – (i) Independent Constraints, (ii) Unidirectional Dependency Constraints, (iii) Bi-directional Dependency Constraints; (iv) Time-dependent-violation Constraints; (v) Exclusions.

B LEVEL II Exclusions: Does the resource under consideration have islands of quantitative exclusions, which if not earmarked, could render the resource fruitless in the market.

B LEVEL III Objective Constraints: Decide which of the quantitative constraints are objective. Usually in (minimally) bi-directional constraints, one is objective barring those attributes, which are completely new global discoveries or inventions.

B LEVEL III Subjective Constraints: Decide which of the quantitative constraints are subjective. Usually in (minimally) bi-directional constraints, one is subjective.

The subjective one decides the life-cycle cost of ownership.

C. QUALITATIVE CONSTRAINTS

C LEVEL I Outer Constraints: Does the thing under consideration undergo change in qualitative properties (physical / chemical / biological / mental) with time? If yes, to what extend is it acceptable? Which of the limits (minimum or maximum or both) to change are mandatory (either or both) by – (i) theory or (ii) law & established standards, or (iii) best local/global practices, making such mandatory limit objective, as it will be applicable on all. All other limits to changes, which are posed internally or individually and are not mandated are completely subjective. Does the thing in question possess this specification, if yes, what is it?

C LEVEL I Inner Constraints: Does the resource assessed need an upgrade in qualitative properties to remain a fruitful resource in market. Upgrade is defined as betterment (as it may be described) of parameters that have been defined by the constraints.

C LEVEL II Constraints: Decide relevant applicable constraints for the attribute assessed. Decide whether applicable LEVEL II constraints are – (i) Independent Constraints, (ii) Unidirectional Dependency Constraints, (iii) Bi-directional Dependency Constraints; (iv) Time-dependent-violation Constraints; (v) Exclusions.

C LEVEL II Exclusions: Does the assessed resource have islands of exclusions in qualitative properties, which should be earmarked to maintain the fruitfulness of resources in market.

C LEVEL III Objective Constraints: Decide which of the qualitative constraints are objective. Usually in (minimally) bi-directional constraints, one is objective barring those attributes, which are completely new global discoveries or inventions.

C LEVEL III Subjective Constraints: Decide which of the qualitative constraints are subjective. Usually in (minimally) bi-directional constraints, one is subjective. The subjective one decides the life-cycle cost of ownership.

D. QUALITATIVE CONSTRAINTS

D LEVEL I Outer Constraints: Does the thing under consideration undergo change in its spatial location or ambience or environs (including geographical location) with time? If yes, is the thing in question, made for working in the ambience and environs or geographical locations? If yes, to what extend is it acceptable? Which of the limits (minimum or maximum or both) to change are mandatory (either or both) by – (i) theory or (ii) law & established standards, or (iii) best local/global practices, making such mandatory limit objective, as it will be applicable on all. All other limits to changes, which are posed internally or individually and are not mandated, are completely subjective. Does the thing in question possess this specification, if yes, what is it?

D LEVEL I Inner Constraints: Does the resource under consideration need a change in its spatial location and/or its operational environs and ambience to remain a fruitful resource in market.

D LEVEL II Constraints: Decide relevant applicable constraints for the attribute assessed. Decide whether applicable LEVEL II constraints are – (i) Independent Constraints, (ii) Unidirectional Dependency Constraints, (iii) Bi-directional Dependency Constraints; (iv) Time-dependent-violation Constraints; (v) Exclusions.

D LEVEL II Exclusions: Does the thing under consideration have islands of exclusions in its location and ambience for operation, so as to remain a fruitful resource in market.

D LEVEL III Objective Constraints: Decide which of the geo-ambience constraints are objective. Usually in (minimally) bi-directional constraints, one is objective barring those attributes, which are completely new global discoveries or inventions.

D LEVEL III Subjective Constraints: Decide which of the geo-ambience constraints are subjective. Usually in (minimally) bi-directional constraints, one is subjective. The subjective one decides the life-cycle cost of ownership.

Most sufficiency conditions have bi-directional (lower and upper; beginning and ending) tolerances of change, some cases have only lower or only upper (Unidirectional), while exceptionally rare cases there are no tolerance limits. A resource without constraints is generally not a resource at all. But we still let an anomaly be in case one is discovered. The author really has not come across a resource with no constraints.

The table on the next page lucidly exhibits all the embodiments of description of an ideal product or service in a tabulated & easy to understand, corroborative form.

10. DNSEA Table

SN	FIELDS	FIELD CATEGORY	FIELD OBJECTIVITY	FIELD CONSTRAINTS	PERMISSIBLE FIELD DIRECTIONS & VALUES		ASSESSMENT TYPE	ASSESSMENT HURDLE
A.	**CATEGORIZATION**							
	Have you experienced analogous resource (Yes / Yes, re-experienceing this, No / No, Re-experiencing this)	N. A.	Subjective	N. A.	Values	Quaternion	Inquired repeatedly	
B.	**ASSESSMENT**							
B.1.	**NECESSARY ATTRIBUTES' FRAMEWORK**							
B.1.1.1.	Safety (Risks). Values are calculated for Risk of declassification of any of the 10 resources including 11 microeconomic resources	Safety	Objective	N. A.	Values	Binary	Once upfront in process	1
B.1.1.2.	Safety (Uncertainties). Plan for responsibility fixing for each of the 10 Resources and 11 microelectronic resources							2
B.1.2.1.	Fitness-in-purpose	Fitness	Objective	N. A.	Values	Binary	Once upfront in process	3
B.1.2.2.	Fitness-in-geoambience							4
B.1.2.3.	Fitness-in-time							5
B.1.2.4.	Fitness-in-cost							6
B.2.	**SUFFICIENCY ATTRIBUTES' FRAMEWORK**							
B.2.1.1.	Resistivity to declassification owing to ownership changes in attributes	Ownership	In all bidirectional attributes one of the two limits are Objective, the other usually subjective	Level I, II — Level III: Usually Bidirectional with Objective & Subjective Constraints	Values & Directions	Multiple	Constant, Regular Monitoring	7
B.2.1.2.	Declassification for lack of essential ownership changes in attributes							7
B.2.2.1.	Resistivity to declassification owing to quantitative changes in attributes	Quantitative						8
B.2.2.2.	Declassification for lack of essential quantitative changes in attributes							8
B.2.3.1.	Resistivity to declassification owing to qualitative changes in attributes	Qualitative						9
B.2.3.2.	Declassification for lack of essential qualitative changes in attributes							9
B.2.4.1.	Resistivity to declassification owing to geoambient changes in attributes	Geo-Ambient						10
B.2.4.2.	Declassification for lack of essential geoambient changes in attributes							10
B.3.	**EMOTIONAL CONNECT (LIKEABILITY) FRAMEWORK**							
B.3.1.1.	Emotional Connect of the Participating Entities	Absolute Emotional Connect	Subjective	N. A.	Values	Binary	Once upfront in process	11
B.3.1.2.	Emotional Connect of the Effected Entities							12
B.3.2.1.	Emotional Connect (Comparative) of the Participating Entities	Comparative Emotional Connect						13
B.3.2.2.	Emotional Connect (Comparative) of the Effected Entities							14
B.4.	**AESTHETICS FRAMEWORK**							
B.4.1.	Absolute Aesthetic (Yes / No / Value)	Aesthetics statistically deduced from Absolute Emotional Connect B.3.1.1. & B.3.1.2.	Objective	Single Constraint - Minimum likeability vote percentage hurdle for Universel likeability	Value	Ternary	Constantly calculated and updated from Emotional connect votes	15
B.4.2.	Comparative Aesthetic (Yes / No / Value)	Aesthetics statistically deduced from Comparative Emotional Connect B.3.2.1. & B.3.2.2.	Objective	Single Constraint - Minimum likeability vote percentage hurdle for Universel likeability	Value	Ternary	Constantly calculated and updated from Emotional connect votes	16

11. DNSEA and Generic Scoring Methodology

Understanding of quality description was a major hurdle in establishing a methodology for generic and correct scoring. This solution to the problem of scoring was more serendipity rather than purposeful.

Once DNSEA was established, methodology for scoring was easy to invent.

Hurdle-Rank	Particulars	Score
1	Unsafe Risks (0.00, 0.10, 0.20,... 0.90 → each denoting one of the ten components* of Risks)	<1.00
2	Safe for creators and users	1.00
3	Fit-for-purpose (or essential absence of it)	1.25
4	Fit-for-geoambience (or essential non-specificity of it)	1.50
5	Fit-for-time (or essential uncertainty of it)	1.75
6	Fit-for-cost (or essential non-assessibility of it)	2.00
7	Ownership or possessional change - either acceptable or unacceptable when within specified constraints	2.25
8	Quantitative change - either acceptable or unacceptable when within specified constraints	2.50
9	Qualitative change - either acceptable or unacceptable when within specified constraints	2.75
10	Geoambience change - either acceptable or unacceptable when within specified constraints	3.00
11	Absolute Emotional Connect of Participating Entities (Doers)	3.00 - 3.25
12	Absolute Emotional Connect of Participating Entities (Orderers)	3.25 - 3.50
13	Comparative Emotional Connect of Effected Entities (Orderers)	3.50 - 3.75
14	Comparative Emotional Connect of Effective Entities (Orderers)	3.75 - 4.00
15	Absolute Aesthetic value (statistical confirmation percentage of absolute emotional connect)	4.00 - 4.50
16	Comparative Aesthetic value (statistical confirmation percentage of absolute emotional connect)	4.50 - 5.00

	* The table indicating value vs risk type (from row 1 of table above) is mentioned below:	Score
i	Microeconomic or business risks	0.00
ii	Socio-Cultural group risks	0.10
iii	Emotional risks	0.20
iv	Academic-Intellectual-Scientific behavioural risks	0.30
v	Administrative & Management Risks	0.40
vi	Politico-legal, macro-economic risks	0.50
vii	Public-health & existential risks	0.60
viii	Technical & Technological risks	0.70
ix	Information, Digital & Cyber Access to data risks	0.80
x	Environmental and Ambient risks	0.90

While there is no mathematics behind claiming the crown of aesthetic value, yet, a proposal is made below, whereby for a specific number of total responses there is a corresponding percentage of likeness responses that is mandated for claiming an object's aesthetics.

Total no. of responses		Min. %age to claim aesthetic value
From	to	
3	10	67%
11	100	70%
101	1,000	75%
1001	10,000	80%
10001	100,000	85%
100001	1,000,000	90%
1000001	10,000,000	92%
10000001	100,000,000	97%
100000001	1,000,000,000	99%

It is important to have a checklist of words (given in next section) that define any meta-stage score. Say 3.00-3.50 could have discipline as 3.10, assertiveness as 3.20 etc. Create the list of words defining Emotional connect of the Doer, Orderer or the aesthetic value, draw a priority list and then describe achievement of each such quality factor with a discrete score. Such words assist in recognizing& adjudging quality.

Hurdle-Rank: Parameters by which quality of tangibles or intangibles is adjudged, are placed in a certain priority. If necessary, sufficient conditions are not met, the Doer & Orderer feel no emotional connect with the produce, what good is the aesthetic value even if, available. Similarly, anything, which is not meeting the sufficiency conditions, will be rated at 2 even if it is aesthetically good and the Doer and Orderer like the produce. The subcategories of emotional connect (likeness), which are not detailed here are devoid of any such priority or need of achieving the first, to make the choice of second valid. It means one may like the smell of something though it might not be visually appreciated.

The next big thing is to train people on scoring quality. This is more difficult. To aid, I decided to prepare a compendium of English words, which may be used for assessing various metrics of quality scoring. Following are the expressions connected with various metrics of quality:

Safety first

Security and safety of the user, Safety of the environment

Fitness for Purpose

Requisition, Technical Specifications, Correctness, Efficiency, Economy, Suitability, Congruence, Compliance, Resource, Conformance, Functionality, Generality, Utilization, Install ability

Sufficiency Conditions

Quantitative Changes (Dimensions, mass, etc.)

Accuracy, interoperability, time, behavior, mental ability, Resilience

Qualitative changes (Change in Properties)

Changeability, Testability, Stability, Reliability, Fault Tolerance, Recoverability, Learnability

Change in owner

Understandability, Reusability

Change in location

Operating conditions, Operational Temperature, Operational Humidity, Operational Pressure, Salinity, Shock & Vibration tolerance, Wind pressure, Dust Tolerance, Acid/Acidity Tolerance, Technical Protections, Used language,

Controversial light, Controversial sound or Controversial words, Perishable

Emotional Connect of the Doer / Orderer
Learn ability, Operability, Analyzability, Adaptability, Usability, Clarity and Understandability, Passion, Patience, Persuasiveness, Convincing, Aggression, Discipline, Remembrance or Recall value, Out-of-the-box thinking, Spatial-Cognition, Intelligence, Wittiness, Attitude, Brevity, Comprehension

Aesthetic Value
Most-voted, Most-popular, Overwhelmingly-liked, Beautiful, Par-excellence, Accurate, Perfection, Chef-d'oeuvre, Peaceful, Calming, Captivating, Melodious, Sublime, Warm, Wise, Positive, Smiling, Happy, Optimistic

These words need to be remembered & brooded upon, while assessing the quality of almost anything from food, to cars, and weather, movies, drama, trains, flights, politicians, language & internet!

Once the concept was ready, I started using it observationally through thought experimentations in various places randomly. Say, I went to a restaurant and evaluated whether could our metrics evaluate the quality of restaurant. I observed that almost everything from marriage to cars to movies can be assessed on these metrics. There could be certain parts of the metric scheme that might not be applicable, but the methodology is applicable in almost every situation. Say in case of a movie, the necessary conditions are clear but the sufficiency conditions are much more difficult for prescription. While there is no change in dimensions, in ownership, or in properties, but change in location (geography) is important there are films like those made in Hollywood, which are more geography neutral then say Bengali cinema. Emotional connect of the doer might be difficult to access (until and unless the actors are interviewed) in cinema, but the emotional connect of the Orderer (which is the viewer) is captured. Now in case of cinema, the <u>remembrance</u> or <u>recall</u> value is important to establish the emotional connect of the Orderer (you will find both these words in the compendium aggregated above of words explaining emotion connect of the Doer/Orderer).

I then arrived to the evident next - Can candidates proposed for hiring, be graded on same metrics? To my surprise I discovered –yes. This is how it works:

Quality definition and the most difficult case – Hiring
Necessary Conditions in hiring: We first list the necessary requirements for a candidate we interview – these could be education, experience, proficiency in certain skills including reading & writing skills. Experience demonstrates that concurrence of a candidate's values with those that an organization propounds is important. These should be one of the necessary conditions for any position.

Sufficiency conditions: The sufficiency conditions prescribe the suitability of the candidate & his skill set, knowledge & learning capability in future as the Co. grows. Skill sets & knowledge is scrutinized to ensure possession of both in areas beyond and besides those, for which one is being interviewed. Additionally, we look at the four constraints, which make a human being - a resource.

Sufficiency - Change in dimensions: In sufficiency conditions concerning dimensions, it might be pertinent to see whether the job that the candidate requires any height/weight/girth/eye-sight/hearing qualifications (example soldiers, pilots, tailors), if yes, they have to be informed in advance of the permissible tolerances in any of such physical requisitions.

Sufficiency - Change in properties: Change in Properties will concur with the minimum level of skills and/or IQ that needs to be possessed for doing a job. Therefore, properties mostly relegate to Capability (as defined earlier in section 'Concept of Resources & Exponential Progress') of a candidate. A good example are professional Pre-Engineering coaching Institutes in India, especially in Kota, where the management arranges full-fledged examinations for the teachers which they are bound to regularly clear, so as to ensure that they are sharp and skillful at problem solving. The property of an employee to learn is also a part of this assessment.

Sufficiency - Change in Geography: Issues generally governed by alteration of geography are following:

(a)   Employees' problem with travelling. Many a times married women staff in Asia show disinclination towards travelling. This needs clarity.

(b)   Local language proficiency has to be considered before posting employees.

(c)   Knowledge of culture, etiquettes, social mores for international postings are critical

Sufficiency - Change in Ownership: Sometimes, certain employees are immobile in their work profile, (here we do not mean change in competency, but only profile). As an example - someone in quality does not want to move from IPQC (In-process quality) to IQC (Incoming quality check). Such employees will not satisfy this condition. Ownership in our case means that of user department.

Emotional Connect of the Doer: This parameter is used to assess the positivity of the candidate towards oneself. It is important to understand as to whether a candidate has satisfaction of doing what he ideally would want to. Is one happy about what one had done earlier or what one may have to do while in job with us. A candidate who is not feeling good about himself, who is not passionate about what he is to do, who is not researching and updating himself in the sphere of his work, is nether disciplined nor happy about his job profile & skill set. Such people do not fulfill this conditionality of possessing emotional connect of the Doer.

Emotional Connect of the Orderer: This attribute exhibits the positivity of the interviewer about the candidate. Does the interviewer feel an emotional connect with the Interviewee? The easiest way to assess this dimension of quality is to evaluate the 'likeness' of the candidate by the assessor. This dimension of assessment is therefore, designed to be completely subjective.

To read more details on emotional connect kindly await publication of Patent on the Invention, which will be available on the author's website.

Aesthetic Value: Is the candidate keeping himself aesthetically-well[20]. Imagine a candidate who meets both necessary and sufficient conditions, he is positive about himself, the interviewer is also positively impressed, but when he gets up to go, one sees him in a business suit on top but in carpet sleepers in feet (assuming there is no special condition mandating him to be in sleepers), he will naturally be incongruent. Such people cannot be called aesthetically good because even if the interviewer likes him, his 'universal likeness' (defined as Aesthetics) is expected to be poor.

Having said the abovementioned, our quality scoring system no how mandates that only those scoring above 3 or 4 should be hired. Some candidates might be extraordinarily overweighed with necessary conditions and sufficiency conditions' completion and one can ignore emotional connect & Aesthetics in favour of the former. This is the interviewer's or hiring departments' choice. Indeed, the Co. has the choice of clearly specifying for each job the minimum score requirement. As an example in product engineers 3 is hirable while in product designers 4 will be mandatory. For the position of an accounts executive whose job is only to make entries in books of accounts a score of 2 might be acceptable, as the job profile does not require depth

---

[20] It is nothing to do with the appearance of any physical deficiency that a candidate might have. If there are some physical requirements to a job then it is mandatory to make them part of the 'fitness for purpose' criteria & not aesthetic value

or growth. It rather requires lots of practice (that is the reason why experience is considered as a necessary condition in hiring). In case of front office executive (receptionist), a score of 4 should be mandatory. Therefore, the Co. can set these conditions for each position that it intends to hire. To make it easier, I published a checklist for interviewers to use with all the aforementioned words. Such scoring saves the Co. from those situations, where the interviewers are not finding the right person for long and at the end of the process decide to hire whosoever best they get. Thereby, compromising extremely important resource of the Co., for flimsy reasons like 'getting late to go back home' or 'hiring pressures'.

This system of interviewing ensures that interviewees are objectively and subjectively assessed. It's recommended that on completion of each stage of assessment – the interviewers compare the score each Interviewer awarded. In ideal situation, the standard deviation should be small. Ideally, words describing a particular score level should be pre-established to ensure objectivity and unanimity.

When such interviews were conducted, it was observed that close to unanimity was achieved on whether to hire any particular candidate or not.

In certain rare cases, we provided candidates special IDs, which made it apparent that the person is a candidate under consideration for hire. We then let them move around the office freely looking at who does what, and how, freely interacting with people who are working (they understand that the said person is a candidate and hence interact with him to provide a feedback). Subsequently, we procure a feedback about the interviewee from all those employees with whom the candidate interacted. While from the candidate we ask questions like – "quote three good & 3 bad things you observed through the day, giving reasons for categorizing them good or bad." Such questions strongly help in understanding people. While the employees provide an equally valuable response, since they now suddenly become interviewers!

Judging the quality of people and scoring them is the most difficult case of utility of our quality concept, judging the quality of products and services using our definition and scoring system is much easier.

If observed, the proposed quality system actually carries both objective and subjective metrics. While necessary (fit-for-purpose conditions & safety conditions) & sufficient conditions (either lower or higher limits of all the four components of sufficiency) for being fit for purpose are objective parts of quality assessment, Emotional Connect is the subjective part, while aesthetic is again close to objective part of the assessment. Such assessment enables comprehensive view of a candidate.

It is worthwhile to note that emotional assessment by virtue of its subjectivity, automatically surfaces on the top. It is obvious since those metrics which are known and are universally[21] & objectively assessable are kept as objective

---

[21] universally known and uniformly understood

criteria, while the subjective emotional assessment for lack of universality are enumerated as the top criteria.

DNSEA, post-training, actually helps people objectify aspects that are often perceived subjective, while making assessment easier owing to a common understanding of assessment metrics. This assumes critical importance in multicultural assessment teams, by socio-culturally degreasing interviewers, who come from varied cultural, linguistic, and economic backgrounds.

Our quality definition and scoring system standardization, makes hiring easy and objective, while making comparison among candidates - simple & apparent. Among all candidates, hire the one, which has best scores. If two candidates have similar scores, hire the one who performs better on sufficiency. If both are equally sufficient, then hire the one who shows higher intellect. If she/he are same in intellect then, for discovery team hire him who is less experienced but a good learner, whereas for the execution team hire him, who has more experience. If two candidates still equate then, for discovery team hire him who is younger, for execution team hire him who is older.

Readers might actually question whether I followed this process while hiring for myself.

In the beginning - No, is the answer. Since all the aforementioned revelations and definitions happened in course of looking for methodologies to do sensible, understandable, and uniform hiring, therefore, I could have not implemented them since beginning. But once the concept was formulated, we went ahead and followed it.

All people hired in last two years have been hired using this quality scoring system that evolved. The desire to have a sensible system in place for hiring is critical because hiring shouldn't be done on basis of the interviewers' experience, and/or gut feels only.

Once we shifted to aforementioned metrics we started to clearly spot the efficiencies and deficiencies of different candidates and those of our qualitative hiring system. I believe we raised the bar on hiring all together.

I therefore resolved for myself major issues –

(a) Standardized quality definition which more or less encompasses all the elements that decide quality, although surely there is enough scope for further improvement, which we intend to do going forward.
(b) Standardized scoring system – now score 0.10, 1 or 2 or 3.00, or 3.25 etc. meant something discrete and were not given by just one factor – likeability which is also a component of our evaluation system, but is not the whole.
(c) Standardized interviewing, hiring, and recruitment, which are the first most important issues for start-ups like ours.

12.   Description of Performance using DNSEA

Of all that I researched, I found 'Performance' as most subterraneous. It is more complicated than it looks at the first glance. Would you consult any of the scores of sites defining performance, it is usually stated to be the level of output vis-à-vis set target/standard.

We have defined performance in a new context – that of our quality definition:

Performance is the quantity and quality of the output of an employee to the set benchmarks or targeted levels. To understand performance thoroughly, we apply my quality definition.

NECESSARY CONDITIONS

Fit for Purpose	Quantity of output as deemed necessary through a candidate's Key Responsibility Areas
Safety First	Not Applicable

SUFFICIENCY CONDITIONS

Sufficiency conditions are actually conditions of sustainability of the quantitative results & is a resistance to declassification of tangible or intangible as a Resource (as defined in our definition before)

- Change in Dimensions

   Growth in the quantity of Absolute Output of an employee vis-à-vis last period

- Change in Properties

  Growth in Sustainability (Repeat-Output/Total-Output)

  Growth in Efficiency

  Growth in Effectiveness

  Growth in Productivity

- Change in Location

  Impact of change in geographical location / department on the performance of the employee

- Change in Ownership

  Impact of change in reporting officer on the performance of the employee

EMOTIONAL CONNECT

Emotional Connect of the Doer

- Subjective self-appraisal of a Candidate

Emotional Connect of the Orderer are:

- Management Appraisal
- Subjective Appraisal of the Customers [Vendor-Supplier for Purchase department; Buyers for Sales & CRM department]

AESTHETIC VALUE

Aesthetics: Evaluation by team members (to remind you – we defined 'Aesthetic' to be 'universal likeness').

As is evident, performance is much more holistic and balanced here than how it is treated usually in business. Like everything else, the definition of quality, when applied to the concept of performance provides for excellent results.

13. DNSEA and Maslow's Theory

Maslow's hierarchy of needs is a theory in psychology proposed by Abraham Maslow in his 1943 paper "A Theory of Human Motivation" in Psychological Review. Maslow subsequently extended the idea to include his observations of humans' innate curiosity. His theories parallel many other theories of human developmental psychology, some of which focus on describing the stages of growth in humans. He then decided to create a classification system, which reflected the universal needs of society as its base and then proceeding to more acquired emotions. Maslow's hierarchy of needs is used to study how humans intrinsically partake in behavioral motivation. This theory is a main base in knowing how effort and motivation are correlated when discussing human behavior. Maslow's theory was fully expressed in his 1954 book Motivation and Personality. The hierarchy remains a very popular framework in sociology research, management training and secondary and higher psychology instruction. Maslow's classification hierarchy has been revised over time. The original hierarchy states that a lower level must be completely satisfied and fulfilled before moving onto a higher pursuit. However, today scholars prefer to think of these levels as continuously overlapping each other. This means that the lower levels may take precedence back over the other levels at any point in time.

The hierarchy needs are well articulated in famed Maslow triangle, which is depicted below:

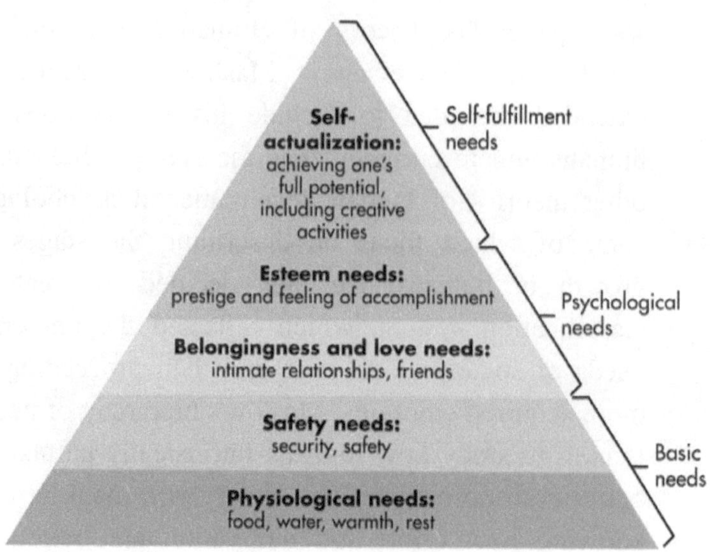

It is interesting to observe the hierarchy & compare it with the hierarchy presented in DNSEA. There are interesting overlaps and some disparities. Which we highlight in this section. The purpose is to redefine Maslow's theory in terms of DNSEA.

I present below slightly changed hierarchy that concurs with DNSEA, and is represented similarly by a triangle.

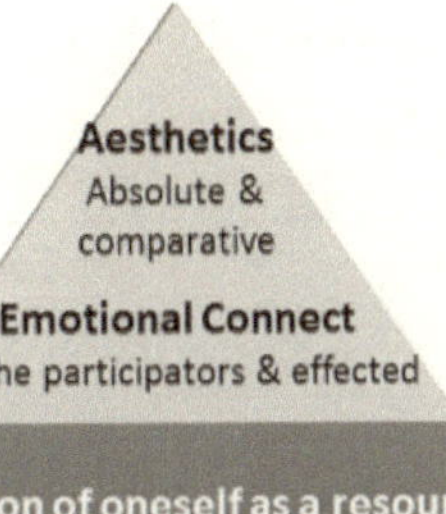

The foremost visible similarity is the five levels of hierarchy common in both.

- The dissimilarity is that Maslow hierarchy is for humans, while DNSEA is for all resources, humans included.

DNSEA and Maslow hierarchies in comparison:

	MASLOW	DNSEA
1	**Psychological Needs** Food, water, warmth, rest	**1 Safety, Security & Risk Management** Ensure that survivability & operability is retained
2	**Safety Needs** Security, Safety	**2 Fitness** By purpose, time, geo-ambience, cost
3	**Belongingness & love needs** Intimate relationships, friends	**3 Resource Longevity** Fruitfulness of a resource.
4	**Esteem Needs** Prestige and feeling of accomplishment	**4 Emotional Connect** Of participating & effected parties
5	**Self Actualization** Achieve one's full potential, including creative activities	**5 Aesthetic Value** Absolute and comparative aesthetics

MASLOW	DNSEA
1 Psychological Needs Food, water, warmth, rest **2 Safety Needs** Security, Safety	**1 Safety, Security & Risk Management** Ensure that survivability & operability is retained
5 Self-Actualization Achieve one's full potential, including creative activities	**2 Fitness** By purpose, time, geo-ambience, cost
	3 Resource Longevity Fruitfulness of a resource.
3 Belongingness & love needs Intimate relationships, friends **4 Esteem Needs** Prestige and feeling of accomplishment	**4 Emotional Connect** Of participating & effected parties
	5 Aesthetic Value Absolute and comparative aesthetics

In view of the aforementioned let us independently do an ideal DNSEA of human life to create a true Maslow like hierarchy that is complete in itself. Thereafter, the disparity amongst the two shall become clear and apparent.

Safety First Framework Attributes for Humans

Risk, as we defined it, is the probability of a resource to be rendered fruitless. The mother of all risks for a human to be rendered fruitless is the risk of losing life. From this risk arise all other including, lack of - food, water, warmth, rest, social connectivity, health etc.

Lack of emotional gratification is also a risk to fruitfulness of a human. Social castigation and being out-casted can also lead to loss of life owing the emotional stress it causes. Loss of political freedom, can lead to societal stresses and loss of life. Loss of consciousness too has similar impact on fruitfulness of life. Similarly, extreme lack of other resources can lead to heightened risks to life and property of humans.

All humans and societies, at large, work for reduction of risks to one's fruitfulness. While undeniably, lack of resources does push one towards high-risk activities, yet given an opportunity aversion to risks that endanger human survival is interwoven genetically into us.

The first two levels of Maslow's hierarchy are actually one and same – they are both related to human need to avoid risk of being disqualified as fruitful resource.

Fitness Framework Attributes for Humans

Need to be fit for Purpose

Humans have four objective purposes that are not sounded aloud, nonetheless, they are present ab-intio. The first is to survive oneself, second one kicks in if the first one fails – that is - to ensure survival of the species.

Third is to be healthy and fit.

The only other attribute of fitness class is - Maslow hierarchy's top level of – 'Self-Actualization'; that is to achieve ones full potential, including creative activities is an overall objective purpose of many. It is only a fitness framework attribute and not the top notch attribute as indicated in Maslow's hierarchy. The reason being that even slaves, and feudal labour would work their days to earn their bread, while at nights they would do art, craft, carving wood, carpentry etc. Self-actualization within the available means and without risking running the risk of being rendered unfruitful resource is inherent and objective salience of humans.

There could be multiple other purposes of lives of humans, but they are all subjective and therefore do not fit in this category, as fit for purpose has to be an objective attribute by definition. We therefore, ignore other subjective attributes, which could be very subjective.

Fitness in time & cost are not applicable to humans. Geo-ambience, I am not sure, while there are certain genetic and racial aspects of humans that prefer specific weather conditions to others, I am afraid to call them fitness conditions.

Interestingly, Maslow has nothing relating to fitness. The reason being that

Sufficiency Attributes:

Sufficiency attributes are a very important aspect of human-life that Maslow's hierarchy has not provided for. This aspect investigates how changes occurring in humans with time makes them better or worse as fruitful resource.

Ownership changes:

Ownership attributes are critical. These who case how participating and effected parties (people) who influence one and get influenced, chisel one as a fruitful resource. Social and family contacts are an important aspect of a human. So, in case the company of a young man changes from constructive to destructive, it will have a major impact on the human concerned.

Quite similarly, people who become leaders have a different track of progress. Such people measure their fruitfulness in the effectiveness with which they can influence others. A leader, who is not followed, ceases to be a fruitful leadership resource.

Quantitative changes:

A human being's changing quantitative attributes like height, weight, eye-sight, change a human's life very dramatically. A good example would be the incapability of a man going obese to be a pilot, irrespective of how much he desires.

Qualitative changes:

A human being's changing qualitative attributes similarly contribute to is fruitfulness as a resource. A person who with time becomes a recluse cannot aspire to be a politician.

Geo-ambience changes:

Geo-ambience is another important change attribute that contributes to fruitfulness of a human as a resource. A person who has lived all his life in northern Europe cannot be effective in tropical areas.

All the aforementioned are important because humans are inclined to better their fruitfulness and in worst-case scenario maintain their levels of fruitfulness as a resource.

Emotional Connect

This is all about likeability, about emotional connect.

A slightly deeper discussion on this is needed. Maslow has dedicated two of his hierarchy levels (Level 3: Belongingness & love needs - Intimate relationships, friends; and Level 4: Esteem Needs, Prestige and feeling of accomplishment) to one and same DNSEA category – Emotional Connect. This aspect of human need description needs more in-depth understanding.

IMPORTANT:

It is human tendency to overrate emotional connect and underrate necessary and sufficiency attributes.

The reason for over-rating emotional connect is that likeability provides an immediate gratification to human mind, as soon as emotional connect information is captured by human senses.

That which is pleasant in smell or touch, looks beautiful, sounds good or is tasty, registers itself immediately in human mind. It provides an endorphin boost to human mind and is addictive.

Humans could sometime ignore even safety risks for that which is emotionally gratifying. There have been enough examples, where mankind has been plunged into wars and destruction for beauty or other emotional gratification.

Sufficiency attributes are often ignored in the face of emotional gratification onslaught. Reason being that issues related to sufficiency are often realized with time. Sufficiency relates to how something changes with time and how it maintains its fruitfulness as a resource. Gratification, if at all, is very gradual and difficult to observe. Understanding of that which does not provide immediate gratification, but pays in the longer run, needs wisdom.

Aesthetic Value

Aesthetic value is a statistical output from emotional connect of people towards oneself. Aesthetic value relates to universal likeability. This aspect is top-most level in DNSEA hierarchy. It relates to the need of a human to be liked and appreciated by all others.

14. DNSEA Case Studies

14.1. DNSEA of Restaurant Food

Necessary Attributes:

Safety First:

> The food should be cooked from fresh and quality ingredients, should be hygienically made, hygienically stored and served.

Fit for purpose:

> While there could be multiple attributes for being fit for purpose (depending on the purpose), yet the minimum would be nutritious, healthy & good to eat.

Sufficiency Attributes:

Change in dimension/quantity:

> Food that inflates is usually that which has been fermented, except for some cheeses, this is not permissible.

Change in properties:

> Food that has changed in its taste, or smell or texture is usually not acceptable as such changes happen because of it going stale. There could be exceptions but this will depend on the food being adjudged.

Change in environs/ambience:

> Interestingly, lot of food is stored frozen. It is important to ensure that such food is not thawed multiple times in its storage cycle, but only once when it is to be cooked.

Change in ownership:

Food is a matter of culture and habit. Therefore, it should be carefully observed whether the food being consumed belongs to the cultural taste palette of the consumer, as otherwise there the food will be adjudged bad owing to a mismatch of the habitual and cultural reasons which are subjective.

Emotional Connect:

Of the doer:

The chefs should have like making the food served.

Of the Orderer:

The consumer should like (no strings attached and no justifications required) the food served.

Aesthetic Value:

If people coming from different cultures, taste palette and habitual backgrounds have appreciated & liked the food, and subject to it meeting the necessary and sufficiency conditions and being liked by the doer and the consumer, it will be termed as aesthetically excellent.

14.2. DNSEA of Marriage

Necessary Attributes:

Safety First:

Bio-compatibility & knowledge of past history of the spouse is important. Mental balance & heterosexuality are important.

Fit for purpose:

Healthy & potent.

Sufficiency Attributes:

Change in dimension/quantity:

Concurring views of spouses on graceful ageing. So that one does not divorce the other for being fat or less active.

Change in properties:

Whether the character, thinking and habits of a spouse have changed for better or worse

Change in environs/ambience:

Whether the spouse has a split personality and changes with change in ambience or holds himself balanced in all environs.

Change in ownership:

Not applicable.

Emotional Connect:

Of the doer:

Does one spouse like other?

Of the Orderer:

Is the liking of the doer reciprocated?

Aesthetic Value:

Do other people – your family, friends and neighbours categorize your union as very good & appreciate it, or not.

14.3. DNSEA of a Perfume

Necessary Attributes:

Safety First:

The bottling of the perfume should be impeccable as most perfumes contain alcohol and can catch fire. This is important as often one travels with these liquids by air.

Fit for purpose:

Good smell

Sufficiency Attributes:

Change in dimension/quantity:

How much perfume is to be sprayed per day? Thereby, defining the time within which 100ml will get consumed.

Change in properties:

How long does the smell retain on one's body. Some perfumes smell excellently but do not survive 15minutes.

Change in environs/ambience:

The perfume should work in users' working climate. If it doesn't one might smell of sweat in a hot summer notwithstanding having used a perfume.

Change in ownership:

Not applicable.

Emotional Connect:

Of the doer:

The user himself should like the smell of the perfume

Of the Orderer:

People who are around you – family or co-workers should appreciate that smell.

Aesthetic Value:

The perfume should be universally recognized as one having enticing smell – which means it is universally liked and appreciated.

14.4. DNSEA of a Printed Circuit Board (PCB)

Necessary Attributes:

Safety First:

The PCB should be created using safe methods. It should have been stored in conditions, which do not transfer static charge to them.

It should undergone all the tests that are recommended on safety.

Fit for purpose:

It should concur with the technical specifications provided by the orderer.

It should have undergone all the tests needed to ensure concurrence with the technical specifications requisitioned by the orderer.

Sufficiency Attributes:

Change in dimension/quantity:

The thickness of the conducting layers has to be uniform and not varying.

The line width of the conductors should also be within the tolerance

Change in properties:

Protective coating to be provided, so that the conducting layer does not react with ambience oxygen and get oxidized with time.

Change in environs/ambience:

Depending on the environment, the nation and the weather where the PCB will be used, it will need to concur with the relevant statutory and technical specifications.

Change in ownership:

> The time of delivery or title change should concur with that agreed in the contract.

Emotional Connect:

> Of the doer:
>
> > The manufacturer is satisfied with the product after all the testing.
>
> Of the Orderer:
>
> > The orderer should be happy with the product after doing all the buyers' tests.

Aesthetic Value:

> > The product is tested by a third party lab and certified as safe and concurring with the requisitioned specifications.

The users shall be free to use the vocabulary provided in previous section of this book. It needs mention that the vocabulary is not all-encompassing and there could be innumerably more words defining the necessary, sufficient attributes as well as emotional connect and aesthetic value. The author provides a methodology, while the users are inspired to discover and create various attributes for each of the event, object, people, phenomena and process under scrutiny.

Kindly provide your reviews about the book on the below mentioned link, else scan the QR to go to the link:

https://www.facebook.com/inventionofdescription

---------------------------∞------------------------